CHOSEN

to excel, inspire, and impact the world for God

SUSIE ADWOA KOFFIE

Chosen

Copyright © 2025 Susie Adwoa Koffie

All rights reserved. No part of this book may be reproduced or transmitted in any form or by any means without the written permission of the author.

Scriptures marked KJV are taken from the KING JAMES VERSION (KJV): KING JAMES VERSION, public domain. Scripture taken from the New King James Version®. Copyright © 1982 by Thomas Nelson. Used by permission. All rights reserved.

Scripture quotations marked (NIV) are taken from the Holy Bible, New International Version®, NIV®. Copyright © 1973, 1978, 1984, 2011 by Biblica, Inc.™ Used by permission of Zondervan.

All rights reserved worldwide. www.zondervan.com. The "NIV" and "New International Version" are trademarks registered in the United States Patent and Trademark Office by Biblica, Inc.™. Scriptures marked AMP are taken from the AMPLIFIED BIBLE (AMP): Scripture taken from the AMPLIFIED® BIBLE, Copyright © 1954, 1958, 1962, 1964, 1965, 1987 by the Lockman Foundation Used by Permission. (www.Lockman.org)

Published by:
Eleviv Publishing Group
Centerville, OH 45458
info@elevivpublishing.com
www.elevivpublishing.com

ISBN:
PB: 978-1-952744-85-3
Ebook: 978-1-952744-86-0

Printed in the United States of America

DEDICATION

This book is solely dedicated to
the MOST-HIGH GOD who led
me to write it and made
everything possible. To Him
ALONE be ALL the Glory, Honor, and Adoration!!

ACKNOWLEDGEMENT

A big thank you to my loving family, whose unwavering support and pillar have been the cornerstone of my journey. Your belief in me and my dreams has been a constant source of inspiration.

To my dearest and precious children, Farida and Hakeem, who have stood by my side through the highs and lows, offering invaluable companionship, wisdom, and unfailing support, I am truly grateful for our deep bond. God bless you beyond measure for all you do. I will ALWAYS love you.

And to all the readers who pick up these pages, may the words within inspire, inform, and ignite your own journey.

With love and gratitude,
Susie Adwoa Koffie (SAK)

TABLE OF CONTENTS

DEDICATION

ACKNOWLEDGEMENT

IN HONOR OF

FOREWORD

ANCHOR SCRIPTURES

CHAPTER 1
WHY GOD CHOSE YOU ………………………………… 13

CHAPTER 2
A DIVINE CALLING-MY PERSONAL JOURNEY ……..… 36

CHAPTER 3
THE CHOSEN APOSTLE PAUL ………….....................… 43

CHAPTER 4
WHY THE CHOSEN SUFFER PERSECUTION ………....... 73

CHAPTER 5
CHOSEN FOR EXPLOITS …..........……………...……... 99

CHAPTER 6
POTENTIAL ROADBLOCKS ………………...............…… 115

CHAPTER 7
SCRIPTURES ON CHOSEN ……………….........………… 130

CHAPTER 8
PRAYERS ON WHY GOD CHOSE YOU ....…….. 152

CHAPTER 9
DECLARATIONS ON CHOSEN ……………………......…… 158

CHAPTER 10
STAY CHOSEN ………............................…………… 172

SALVATION PRAYER

IN HONOR OF
DR. CHARLES STANLEY

This book is written in honor of Dr. Charles Frazier Stanley, a man of God whose teachings immensely impacted my spiritual journey and walk with Christ. In recognition of his remarkable qualities, achievements, teachings, and contributions to my life and the body of Christ. This book is a tribute to his enduring legacy. May the words within these pages serve as a humble homage to his indelible impact on our lives and the world.

With deep respect and admiration,
Susie Adwoa Koffie (SAK)

FOREWORD

In a world that often measures worth by external achievements, societal standards, and momentary success, we must anchor our identity in the truth that we are chosen by God. This divine selection is not a matter of chance but a purposeful act of love that reveals our inherent value and significance.

The Bible affirms our worth as God's chosen people. In 1 Peter 2:9, we read, "But you are a chosen people, a royal priesthood, a holy nation, God's special possession." This powerful declaration reminds us that we are not just random beings but also cherished and set apart by God. Our value is not determined by what we do but by who we are in Him.

Understanding our value begins with recognizing that we were created intentionally. Psalm 139:14 states, "I praise you because I am fearfully and wonderfully made; your works are wonderful, I know that full well." Each of us has been crafted with care, and endowed with unique gifts and talents that reflect God's creativity and purpose. We can embrace the truth that we are inherently valuable when we see ourselves through this lens.

Moreover, being chosen by God comes with a divine purpose. Ephesians 2:10 affirms this: "For we are God's handiwork, created in Christ Jesus to do good works, which God prepared in advance for us to do." Our lives are not accidental, as they are designed with intention. We are called to fulfill specific roles in God's kingdom, impacting the lives of those around us in ways that only we can.

However, the enemy often seeks to undermine our sense of value, whispering lies that we are unworthy or incapable. In those moments, it's essential to remember Romans 8:31, which proclaims, "If God is for us, who can be against us?" Our value is fortified by the knowledge that the Creator of the universe, the Almighty God Himself, stands with us, empowering us to fulfill our purpose despite our fears and insecurities.

As we walk in the knowledge of our value as God's chosen ones, we must also embrace our calling to serve and love others. Galatians 5:13 encourages us, saying, "You, my brothers and sisters, were called to be free. But do not use your freedom to indulge the flesh; rather, serve one another humbly in love." Our purpose is not only self-fulfillment but also reflecting God's love and grace to the world.

I believe that knowing your value as a chosen

vessel by God is a transformative realization. It empowers you to live boldly, pursue your God-given purpose, and impact the lives of others. Let the truth of your worth in Christ echo in your heart as you embrace the unique calling He has placed upon your life. Remember, you are chosen, you are valued, and you are beloved. Embrace it, and let it guide you as you fulfill your purpose in this world. You can accomplish much more than you think. You are stronger than you think. You are more anointed and favored than you think. You are more talented than you think. The dreams and gifts God put in you are much bigger than you think. If you are going to see the fullness of what is in you and why God chose you, you must see yourself the right way.

As you turn these pages, I pray you will be filled with a renewed sense of purpose and a deeper understanding of your identity in Christ. Accept Jesus Christ as your Lord and Personal Savior and develop an intimate and deep relationship with Him. He has the Blueprint for your life, so begin to ask Him questions in prayer about what He has chosen you to do. Ask Him to give you ideas, help restructure your life, and impact the world as the chosen vessel of Christ. May the truths within this book inspire you to embrace the calling upon your life and step into the fullness of what it means to be truly chosen by God.

Happy & Fulfilled Reading,
Susie Adwoa Koffie (SAK)

ANCHOR SCRIPTURES

*But ye are a chosen generation, a royal priesthood, an holy nation, a peculiar people; that ye should show forth the praises of him who hath called you out of darkness into his marvelous light." **(1 Peter 2:9) KJV***

John 15:16 (NIV): *"You did not choose me, but I chose you and appointed you so that you might go and bear fruit—fruit that will last—and so that whatever you ask in my name the Father will give you."*

Matthew 22:14 (ESV): *"For many are called, but few are chosen."*

| CHAPTER 1 |

Why God Chose You

Have you ever wondered why God chose you? Why, out of the billions of souls on this earth, He singled you out and called you by name? It's a question that has perplexed and humbled the hearts of many seekers of faith. God chose us for a purpose and sent us for a purpose. Everyone born of Christ has been selected or chosen for a purpose. You may have been feeling that you were not purposeful before but because you have been redeemed, you have been taken out of darkness like it has been written in the same 1 Peter 2:9: *"that ye should show forth the praises of him who hath called you out of darkness into his marvelous light."*

God has chosen you, and this divine selection is not ordinary. It is rooted in His perfect love and purpose. Understanding why God chose you is crucial to realizing your identity and worth in Him. God's choice is deeply embedded in His Sovereignty. Before the foundation of the world, He knew you and called you by name. Ephesians 1:4-5 states, *"For he chose us in him before the creation of the world to be holy and blameless in his sight. In love, he predestined us for adoption to sonship through Jesus Christ, in accordance with his pleasure and will."* This passage reveals that God's decision to choose you was made long before you took your first breath. It signifies that you were on His mind, intricately designed to fulfill a unique purpose.

The concept of being chosen is not merely theological but personal. God's choice signifies a relationship where you are not just a number in His creation but a beloved child. He desires a connection with you that reflects His love and grace. This truth should fill your heart with awe and gratitude, knowing that you are held in the highest regard by the Creator of the universe.

Understanding that God chose you is also about recognizing the purpose He has for your life. Jeremiah 29:11 assures us, *"For I know the plans I have for you,"* declares the Lord, *"plans to prosper you and not to harm you, plans to give you hope and a future."* This scripture emphasizes that God's choice comes with a blueprint for your life. He has specific plans that are meant to bring you fulfillment and joy.

God has equipped you with unique gifts, talents, and experiences that align with His divine purpose. Whether you are called to serve in your community, support your family, or engage in ministry, your life is a canvas upon which God is painting a masterpiece. When you embrace your role as God's chosen, you begin to see how every good and bad experience contributes to the greater picture of God's plan for you.

God's choice is a manifestation of His love. Romans 5:8 beautifully illustrates this: *"But God demonstrates his own love for us in this: While we were still sinners, Christ died for us."* This profound act of love underscores that God's choice is not based on our worthiness or righteousness, but rather on His unconditional love.

Understanding that you are chosen despite your flaws and failures liberates you from the burden of perfectionism. God values you for who you are, not what you do. This truth invites you to rest in His grace and allows you to approach Him with confidence, knowing that you are accepted and cherished.

Being chosen also means being empowered to fulfill God's purpose. Acts 1:8 declares, *"But you will receive power when the Holy Spirit comes on you; and you will be my witnesses in Jerusalem, and in all Judea and Samaria, and to the ends of the earth."* When God chooses you, He also equips you with the Holy Spirit, who guides, empowers, and strengthens you to carry out His mission.

The Holy Spirit ignites your passion, providing you with the courage and wisdom to navigate life's challenges. Whether you share the Gospel, serve others, or simply live out your faith, the Holy Spirit enables you to impact the world around you. Your choice to rely on His power is essential in fulfilling the purpose God has for your life.

To fully understand why God chose you, it is vital to embrace your identity as His beloved child. Galatians 3:26-28 affirms, *"So in Christ Jesus you are all children of God through faith, for all of you who were baptized into Christ have clothed yourselves with Christ. There is neither Jew nor Gentile, neither slave nor free, nor is there male and female, for you are all one in Christ Jesus."* This passage emphasizes that your identity transcends societal labels and divisions.

As a chosen child of God, you are part of a larger family, a community of believers united in faith. This identity calls you to live in a way that reflects God's love, grace, and mercy to those around you. It invites you to engage in relationships that uplift, encourage, and support one another in the pursuit of God's purpose.

As you reflect on why God chose you, let it reshape your understanding of your value and purpose. You are chosen, loved, and equipped to fulfill a divine calling. Embrace this identity wholeheartedly and walk confidently knowing that your life is a testament to God's incredible grace and love. Remember, you are not alone on this journey but part of a more remarkable story. A story that God has been weaving since the beginning of time. Let this truth empower you to live with purpose, passion, and the assurance that you are chosen for such a time as this.

The words of Jesus in John 15:16, where He states, *"You did not choose me, but I chose you and appointed you so that you might go and bear fruit—fruit that will last."* This simple yet powerful statement speaks volumes about our relationship with God and the purpose He has for each of us.

When we consider the concept of being chosen, we must first recognize that it is not merely a matter of selection but a divine appointment. God, in His infinite wisdom, has chosen each of us for a specific purpose. Just as He chose the disciples to spread the Gospel and establish the early church, He has chosen you and me to fulfill His mission on earth.

Consider the example of Moses in Exodus 3. God chose Moses to lead the Israelites out of bondage in Egypt. Despite Moses' initial reluctance and feelings of inadequacy, God reassured him, saying, *"I will be with you"* (Exodus 3:12). Similarly, God has chosen you, not because of your qualifications, but because of His desire to work through you for His Glory.

Being chosen also signifies belonging. In Ephesians 1:4-5, Paul writes, *"For he chose us in him before the creation of the world to be holy and blameless in his sight. In love, He predestined us for adoption to sonship through Jesus Christ."* This passage reveals that our choice in Christ is rooted in love and acceptance.

Think about the story of Ruth. She was not an Israelite by birth, yet she chose to remain with her mother-in-law Naomi, saying, *"Where you go, I will go, and where you stay, I will stay. Your people will be my people and your God my God"* (Ruth 1:16). Ruth's choice to embrace Naomi's people and God led to her being included in the lineage of Christ. When God chooses us, He invites us into a family of community of believers where we belong.

Being chosen comes with responsibility. Jesus says, *"I chose you and appointed you so that you might go and bear fruit."* This appointment is not passive, as it requires action on our part. We are called to actively participate in God's work and bear fruit that reflects His character.

In Matthew 25:14-30, Jesus shares the Parable of the Talents, illustrating how servants were entrusted with varying amounts of money according to their abilities. The expectation was clear as they were to invest in what they had been given. When the master returned, he rewarded those who had been diligent and fruitful, while the one who buried his talent faced consequences. This parable reminds us that our responsibility as chosen ones is to use our gifts and resources for God's Kingdom.

Being chosen does not mean we are left to our own devices; rather, we are empowered by the Holy Spirit. Acts 1:8 declares, *"But you will receive power when the Holy Spirit comes on you; and you will be my witnesses."* The Holy Spirit equips us to fulfill our calling, guiding us in our actions and decisions.

Consider the early disciples. After Jesus' ascension, they were filled with the Holy Spirit at Pentecost and empowered to preach boldly despite persecution. Their lives bore lasting fruit as they spread the Gospel and established the church. When we rely on the Holy Spirit, we, too, can bear lasting fruit.

The fruit we are called to bear is not just about numbers or outward success, but the character of Christ manifested in our lives. Galatians 5:22-23 outlines the fruit of the Spirit: love, joy, peace, patience, kindness, goodness, faithfulness, gentleness, and self-control. These qualities should be evident in our interactions with others.

For example, the story of the Good Samaritan (Luke 10:25-37) exemplifies the fruit of kindness and compassion. Despite social prejudices, the Samaritan chose to help a wounded stranger, demonstrating that our fruitfulness stems from our willingness to love and serve others, regardless of their background.

As chosen ones, we are also called to make disciples. The Great Commission in Matthew 28:19-20 commands us to *"go therefore and make disciples of all nations."* This responsibility to share the Gospel and nurture others in their faith is a direct result of being chosen.

Consider the story of Philip and the Ethiopian eunuch in Acts 8:26-40. Philip was directed by the Holy Spirit to approach the eunuch, who was reading Scripture but needed guidance. Philip's obedience led to the eunuch's baptism and transformation. Our willingness to share the Gospel can lead to eternal fruit as we help others come to know Christ.

Let us remember the profound truth that we are chosen by God. You did not choose Him; He chose you. This choice is rooted in love, purpose, and responsibility. Embrace your identity as a chosen one and live out your calling with passion and purpose.

Let us bear fruit that lasts, reflecting Christ's character in our lives and actively participating in His mission. May the Holy Spirit empower us to fulfill the great calling placed upon us. Remember, you are chosen, and that makes all the difference. Amen!

1 Peter 2:9 states, *"But you are a chosen people, a royal priesthood, a holy nation, God's special possession, that you may declare the praises of him who called you out of darkness into his wonderful light."* This powerful declaration speaks to our identity as believers and the divine purpose that accompanies it.

To grasp the fullness of our identity as a chosen people, we must first understand what it means to be chosen by God. The phrase *"you are a chosen people"* signifies a deliberate selection. God has not simply picked us ordinarily. He has chosen us for a specific purpose and relationship.

In Deuteronomy 7:6, God tells the Israelites, *"For*

you are a people holy to the Lord your God. The Lord your God has chosen you out of all the peoples on the face of the earth to be his people, his treasured possession." This choice was not based on their merit but on God's love and covenant faithfulness. Similarly, we are chosen not because of our righteousness but because of God's grace.

Being chosen by God signifies an invitation to a deep, personal relationship with Him. In John 15:15, Jesus says to His disciples, "I no longer call you servants, because a servant does not know his master's business. Instead, I have called you friends." This shift from servant to friend illustrates the intimacy of our relationship with God. We are not merely subjects in His kingdom but beloved children and cherished friends.

The story of David exemplifies this relationship. In 1 Samuel 16, God chose David as king, not because of his outward appearance but because of his heart *(1 Samuel 16:7)*. David's relationship with God was characterized by prayer, worship, and an earnest pursuit of God's presence. As chosen people, we are invited into a similar relationship to seek God sincerely and intimately.

Being chosen comes with a calling to live a

life set apart for God's glory. The phrase *"a royal priesthood"* in 1 Peter 2:9 signifies that we are called to represent God to the world and mediate between God and humanity. As priests, we are to embody holiness in our daily lives, reflecting God's character in our actions and attitudes.

In Leviticus 20:26, God commands the Israelites, "You are to be holy to me because I, the Lord, am holy." This call to holiness is echoed in the New Testament as well. In 1 Thessalonians 4:7, Paul writes, *"For God did not call us to be impure, but to live a holy life."* Our identity as a chosen people obligates us to pursue a life that honors God and reflects His purity.

Being part of a royal priesthood also means we are called to serve others. In Mark 10:45, Jesus exemplifies this when He states, *"For even the Son of Man did not come to be served, but to serve."* Our identity as chosen people compels us to follow Christ's example, serving our communities and loving those around us.

The story of the Good Samaritan *(Luke 10:25-37)* illustrates this principle beautifully. Despite societal barriers, the Samaritan chose to help a wounded traveler, demonstrating that our call to service transcends race, religion, and social status. As chosen people, we are called to love and serve others, reflecting Christ's compassion in a world that desperately needs it.

The latter part of *1 Peter 2:9* states, *"that you may declare the praises of him who called you out of darkness into his wonderful light."* Our identity as chosen people comes with a purpose to proclaim God's goodness and glory. We are called to share the story of our salvation and the transformative power of Christ in our lives.

In Psalm 107:2, the psalmist writes, *"Let the redeemed of the Lord tell their story—those he redeemed from the hand of the foe."* This call to declare God's praises is not just for the spiritually elite but for every believer. Your story of redemption is a testimony of God's grace; sharing it can inspire others to seek Him.

Our lives should reflect the light of Christ, serving as a witness to those around us. In Matthew 5:14-16, Jesus calls us the *"light of the world,"* instructing us to let our light shine before others so that they may see our good deeds and glorify our Father in heaven.

Consider the example of the early church in Acts. After Pentecost, the disciples boldly proclaimed the Gospel, resulting in thousands coming to faith. Their lives were a testament to Christ's transformative power. As chosen people, we are called to live in such a way that our actions draw others to Christ, declaring His praises through our words and deeds.

Let us take to heart the truth that we are chosen people. This identity carries immense significance, calling us to a relationship with God, a life of holiness, and a commitment to serving others. More importantly, it empowers us to declare the praises of the One who called us out of darkness into His marvelous light.

Let us embrace our identity as God's special possession and live out our calling passionately and purposefully. May our words and actions reflect His glory, drawing others into the light of His love. Remember, you are chosen; that truth should inspire you to live boldly for Christ. Amen!

As I reflect on a profound truth in Matthew 22:14, where Jesus states, *"For many are called, but few are chosen."* This statement concludes the Parable of the Wedding Banquet, which illustrates God's invitation to salvation and the seriousness of responding to that call.

The call of God is universal. Matthew 22 opens with a parable where the king invites guests to a wedding feast for his son. This invitation represents God's call to all humanity to enter into a relationship with Him. In 2 Peter 3:9, we read, *"The Lord is not slow in keeping his promise, as some understand slowness. Instead, he is patient with you, not wanting anyone to perish, but everyone to come to repentance."* This illustrates God's desire for all people to respond to His invitation.

Consider the story of Jonah. God called Jonah to Nineveh to preach repentance to its people. Initially, Jonah resisted, but eventually, he obeyed, and the entire city turned to God *(Jonah 3:10)*. This story demonstrates that God's call reaches even the most unlikely individuals and places. His invitation is extended to everyone, regardless of their past or background.

The call from God is not merely an invitation to attend an event. It is a call to enter a relationship with Him. In John 15:15, Jesus states, *"I no longer call you servants, because a servant does not know his master's business. Instead, I have called you friends."* This highlights that God desires an intimate relationship with us, where we grow in understanding and fellowship with Him.

When God calls us, He also calls us to a purpose. Ephesians 2:10 tells us, *"For we are God's handiwork, created in Christ Jesus to do good works, which God prepared in advance for us to do."* We are not just called to be passive recipients but to actively participate in His work on earth.

While many are called, few are chosen. This distinction can be perplexing. To be chosen implies a deeper level of commitment and responsibility. In the context of the wedding feast, the guests who refused to come represent those who hear the call but do not respond appropriately.

In 1 Corinthians 1:26-27, Paul writes, *"Brothers and sisters, think of what you were when you were called. Not many of you were wise by human standards; not many were influential; not many were of noble birth. But God chose the foolish things of the world to shame the wise."* This passage reveals that God's choice often defies human expectations. He chooses those who may seem unlikely to be bearers of His message and purpose.

Being chosen also means being set apart. As 1 Peter 2:9 states, we are a *"chosen people, a royal priesthood, a holy nation."* This designation calls us to a life of holiness and transformation. The chosen are expected to reflect Christ's character in their lives.

Take the example of the Apostle Paul. Initially, he was a persecutor of Christians, but after a dramatic encounter with Christ on the road to Damascus *(Acts 9)*, he became one of the most influential apostles. His transformation illustrates that being chosen often involves a radical change and a commitment to God's purpose.

The first step in responding to God's call is acceptance. Just as those invited to the wedding feast had to accept the invitation, we must choose to accept God's invitation into a relationship with Him. This involves faith and a willingness to turn away from our old ways.

In Luke 14:15-24, Jesus tells another parable about a great banquet. Those invited made excuses for not attending, highlighting the reality that many will reject the call. Our acceptance is not just a momentary decision but an ongoing commitment to pursue God daily.

Once we accept the invitation, we must live in a way that reflects our chosen status. This means embodying the values of the Kingdom of God. Philippians 1:27 encourages us to *"conduct yourselves in a manner worthy of the gospel of Christ."* Our lives should demonstrate Christ's love, grace, and truth to those around us.

Consider the example of Esther. She was chosen to be queen for such a time as this *(Esther 4:14)*. When her people faced destruction, she had to act courageously, risking her own life to save them. Esther's response to her calling illustrates that being chosen often requires boldness and action.

Finally, being chosen means we are called to bear fruit. In John 15:16, Jesus says, *"You did not choose me, but I chose you and appointed you so that you might go and bear fruit—fruit that will last."* Our lives should produce lasting impact and reflect the nature of Christ.

The parable of the talents *(Matthew 25:14-30)* illustrates this principle well. Each servant was given a certain amount of money to invest while their master was away. The servants who invested wisely were rewarded, while the one who buried his talent faced consequences. This Bible story teaches us that we must actively use what God has given us to advance His kingdom.

Let us reflect on the profound truth that many are called, but few are chosen. God has extended His invitation to each of us, desiring a relationship that transforms us and empowers us to live out His purpose.

Being chosen comes with responsibility, calling us to accept the invitation, live as representatives of Christ, and bear fruit for His Kingdom. Let us not take this call lightly but instead, let us embrace our identity as chosen people and fulfill the purpose God has laid before us.

May we respond to His call with open hearts and willing spirits, ready to declare His glory and share His love with the world. Amen.

You are not who you used to be; you are new because you have been selected. *"Therefore, if any man be in Christ, he is a new creature: old things are passed away; behold, all things are become new."* 2 Corinthians 5:17

The purpose God chose us is to bless us. You have been selected for blessing, you are a royal priesthood, and you are peculiar. Joshua was chosen to lead the Israelites, and he did great things. At the very core of God's choice is His boundless and unconditional love for each of His children. He doesn't choose us based on our merit or accomplishments. Instead, His love for us is unchanging, unwavering, and independent of our flaws and failures. In His eyes, you are a masterpiece, created with love and destined for greatness.

God's choice is intricately connected to His unique plan for your life. He knows the path you are meant to walk, the challenges you will face, and the victories you will achieve. He chose you because He knows you are the perfect vessel for the mission He has entrusted to you. Your life has a purpose that only you can fulfill.

When God chooses you, He sees who you are and who you can become in Christ. His choice is an invitation to grow, transform, and become more like Jesus. You are capable of far more than you could ever imagine through His grace and power.

God's choice is not an isolated event. It is an invitation to join a community of believers, to be part of a more incredible tapestry of faith. Your unique gifts, experiences, and journey are meant to enrich and strengthen the body of Christ. Together, we are His chosen people, called to reflect His love and light to the world.

Ultimately, God chooses you for His Glory. Your life becomes a living testament to His grace and power. When others see your journey, they should see a reflection of God's love and faithfulness. Your story becomes a testimony of His goodness, a beacon of hope to a world in need.

So, as you contemplate why God chose you, remember that His choice is a declaration of His love, a revelation of His purpose, and an invitation to walk in faith. You are chosen not because you are perfect but because you are loved. Embrace this truth, and let it guide you on your faith journey.

Here are some examples of people whom God

called and chose in the Bible:
- God called Moses from a burning bush to lead the Israelites out of Egypt. Despite Moses' initial reluctance, God empowered him to perform miracles and lead His people to freedom.
- God called Abraham to leave his homeland and become the father of a great nation. Through his faith, Abraham became the patriarch of the Israelites and a model of trust in God's promises.
- God chose David, a shepherd boy, to be the king of Israel. Despite his humble beginnings, David became a renowned leader and the author of many Psalms in the Bible.
- Mary, a young woman from Nazareth, was chosen by God to be the mother of Jesus Christ. Her willingness to accept this divine calling is celebrated as an example of faith and obedience.
- Originally known as Saul, Paul persecuted Christians until he had a life-changing encounter with Jesus on the road to Damascus. God called him to be an apostle to the Gentiles, and he went on to write numerous letters (epistles) in the New Testament.
- God called Jeremiah to be a prophet to the nations. Despite facing opposition and rejection, he faithfully delivered God's messages, earning him the nickname

"the weeping prophet."
- God placed Esther in a strategic position as queen to save the Jewish people from a plot to annihilate them. Her courage and intervention are celebrated in the Book of Esther.
- God chose Noah to build an ark and save his family and animals from a worldwide flood—Noah's obedience to God's calling preserved life on Earth.
- Joseph was sold into slavery by his brothers, and he rose to prominence in Egypt and eventually saved his family during a severe famine.
- Elijah was a prophet who performed many miracles and challenged the false prophets of Baal, demonstrating God's power.
- Daniel was taken into captivity in Babylon. Due to his unwavering faith in God, he interpreted dreams and survived the lion's den.
- God chose Samuel as a young boy, he became a prophet and the last judge of Israel. He anointed both Saul and David as kings.
- Peter was a disciple of Jesus who was chosen to become a leader in the early Christian church, performing miracles and spreading the Gospel.

These biblical examples showcase a diverse range of individuals whom God called and chose for specific purposes. Their stories reflect themes of faith, obedience, and God's sovereignty in selecting ordinary people to accomplish extraordinary things according to His divine plan.

I believe that God chose each of us for a specific purpose. You are a carefully chosen strand, handpicked by the Almighty God, the Creator of the universe, for a particular purpose. Just as He chose Moses to lead His people out of Egypt, David to be a king, and Mary to be the mother of His Son, He has chosen you for a purpose uniquely your own. God's choice is not based on our qualifications, our status, or our past. It is grounded in His divine wisdom and unconditional love. He saw something in you, something He placed there, a spark of potential waiting to be ignited. You might wonder, "Why me? What could I possibly offer?" These are natural questions, but they miss the point. God's choice is not about what you can do but what He can do through you. He looks beyond your limitations and sees the limitless possibilities of a life surrendered to His will.

Your purpose may not be as prominent as those in the Bible, but it is no less significant. Perhaps you are called to be a loving parent to a sick child, a faithful friend, a compassionate neighbor to an elderly person, or a dedicated worker. Each role is a piece of the puzzle, a vital part of God's plan to bring His love and light to the world.

Remember, God doesn't make mistakes. You are not an afterthought but a deliberate creation. The Master Designer has orchestrated your talents, experiences, and story. Your life is not a series of accidents but a divine masterpiece in progress.

So, as you journey through life, embrace the truth that God chose you with a purpose. Seek His guidance, open your heart to His leading, and trust that He will equip you for the tasks He has prepared for you. Your life is a story waiting to unfold, a purpose waiting to be realized, and a calling waiting to be answered.

In every moment, in every choice, remember that you are chosen by God for a specific purpose. Let this knowledge fill you with hope, courage, and a deep sense of meaning. Embrace your divine calling, for you are not here by chance but by divine appointment.

| CHAPTER 2 |

A Divine Calling: My Personal Journey

There comes a moment in life when you realize that you are not just a product of random chance but a result of God's divine design from Heaven. That moment was a turning point, an awakening to the profound truth that God had chosen me for a unique purpose. It happened during a season of uncertainty and self-doubt. I found myself at a crossroads, grappling with questions about my identity, my worth, and my path in life. Amid this inner turmoil, I encountered a series of events that left no doubt in my mind that God had chosen me.

One of the most significant moments was a chance encounter with a stranger who was a pastor who found me sitting behind a store covered with clothes on the outskirts of Makola market in Accra, Ghana. He had no eye contact with me but came to pray over the store, and as he left, the Spirit of the Lord asked him to deliver a message to me. He came to tell me that God had chosen me to do His work, and it would be very soon. He did not know that I had a series of revelations and dreams where God showed me that, but I was still asking Him questions. I did not know then that when God has an assignment for you, He doesn't always give you all the details. He tests your obedience, and as you obey Him and you start to walk in his divine will, the other details fall into place.

One of the many encounters that stood out was a vivid dream I had. In it, I was in line with many others, waiting for our clipboards to be assigned to us for our daily work. When it was my turn, my clipboard had LUKE 10 boldly written on it, and I woke up. I was stunned when I turned to the pages of Luke 10 in the Bible. The story starts with God appointing 70 evangelists to deliver His message in every city and place.

> Luke 10:1-11 KJV: *"After these things the LORD appointed other seventy also and sent them two and two before his face into every city and place, whither he himself would come.*

² Therefore said he unto them, the harvest truly is great, but the laborers are few: pray ye therefore the Lord of the harvest, that he would send forth laborers into his harvest.

³ Go your ways: behold, I send you forth as lambs among wolves.

⁴ Carry neither purse, nor scrip, nor shoes: and salute no man by the way.

⁵ And into whatsoever house ye enter, first say, Peace be to this house.

⁶ And if the son of peace be there, your peace shall rest upon it: if not, it shall turn to you again.

⁷ And in the same house remain, eating and drinking such things as they give: for the laborer is worthy of his hire. Go not from house to house.

⁸ And into whatsoever city ye enter, and they receive you, eat such things as are set before you:

⁹ And heal the sick that are therein, and say unto them, the kingdom of God is come nigh unto you.

¹⁰ But into whatsoever city ye enter, and they receive you not, go your ways out into the streets of the same, and say,

¹¹ Even the very dust of your city, which cleaveth on us, we do wipe off against you: notwithstanding be ye sure of this, that the kingdom of God is come nigh unto you." Luke 10:1-11 KJV.

After I prayed and reflected on Luke 10, I understood my assignment better. I figured that Jesus knew that the time before His crucifixion was short when He sent the seventy out and that many villages had not yet heard His message. Jesus turned to this larger group of His disciples to be His messengers, to prepare these places ahead of Him, and that was what He was asking me to do. I shouldn't be silent but go and announce Him to the world.

This reminded me that there was a larger group of interested followers of Jesus who Jesus was calling to do His work. Jesus chose these seventy to see the glory of God in action as they served and represented Him. Jesus showed these were the ones to "translate" His word into everyday life.

I also noticed that the Bible did not list the names of the 70, so I knew it was better to be one of the unnamed seventy, who did their work and were very happy in it and whose names are only known to God. It was perhaps safer, too, that Judas was among the twelve, but we never read of one among the seventy.

I pondered over Luke 10 several times, trying to understand why God had given that to me and why

Luke 10:2 did something to me. *"Therefore, said he unto them, the harvest truly is great, but the laborers are few pray ye, therefore, the Lord of the harvest, that he would send forth laborers into his harvest."* Luke 10:2 KJV

The harvest is truly great, so pray that the Lord will send laborers into His harvest. This clarified my doubt, and I understood that God had chosen me to make the principles of Jesus' commission my own.

When Jesus said the laborers are few, He meant that there must be more workers and that those engaged in the work must have an appropriate focus on their work. When there is a lot of work and fewer workers, one must be busy with the work. This is a harvest that needs laborers. The goods of a harvest can go to waste if no laborers take advantage of the bounty. Jesus warned us that opportunities to meet human needs and bring people into His kingdom may be wasted because of a shortage of laborers. Jesus commanded them to pray as the work before them was great and could not be accomplished without much prayer. Specifically, they were to ask the Lord of the harvest to send out laborers into His harvest. This speaks powerfully to the fact that Jesus commanded them to have a certain kind of heart, trust God, and not seek to abuse and manipulate others.

Going as lambs among wolves doesn't sound very attractive yet; it was exactly how Jesus was sent and how the power of God worked through Him mightily.

As I delved deeper into my faith and sought God's guidance through prayer and meditation, I began to discern a purpose emerging from the visions and dreams that God gave me. I realized that my experiences, my passions, and my unique set of skills were not accidental but intentional. Through God's gentle promptings and unmistakable signs, I was led down a path of service and ministry I had never considered before. God led me to set up a midnight-hour prayer line. It was a tough assignment for me as I have a full-time job, and I contemplated it and asked God how many days a week I heard daily. The assignment was beyond me, but I had to be obedient to the call. It was as though doors began to open, opportunities presented themselves, and a sense of calling grew stronger with each passing day. The doubts and fears that once held me captive began to lose their grip. Instead, I found myself filled with a newfound confidence and a deep sense of peace. I understood that God's choice was not based on my qualifications or past mistakes but on His unfathomable love and divine plan.

Over time, He led me to write my first book,

"Intimacy with Christ Jesus," and I came to embrace my calling not as a burden but as a privilege. I realized that being chosen by God was not about personal glory but about becoming a vessel through which His love and grace could flow to others. I believe that part of my calling is to write books and use them as a form of Evangelism to share God's word and encourage others in this walk of faith.

My journey is imperfect, and I continue to face challenges and uncertainties. However, the knowledge that God chose me for a specific purpose sustains me through the storms of life. It reminds me that I am part of a more remarkable story woven into the fabric of His divine will.

In my calling, I have found a profound sense of meaning and fulfillment that transcends the ups and downs of this world. I am not just a random existence but a chosen instrument in the hands of a loving Creator, and I am eternally grateful for that.

| CHAPTER 3 |

THE CHOSEN APOSTLE PAUL

So, I now understand why the Spirit of the Lord has made me study the Apostle Paul like no other Apostle in all these years. I didn't know that some time along the line, I was going to be writing a book CHOSEN, and He would have me dedicate a whole chapter to Him. So, I'm writing about Him on April 20th, 2024, a Saturday morning. As I spend time with God and listen to a message, the Holy Spirit drops to dedicate a chapter of this book to Apostle Paul, explaining why He was Chosen and what He accomplished. I am all beaming with smiles and very excited about this because if you have ever done a Bible study with me, then you know how I am passionate about Apostle Paul and about Acts chapter 9, which describes vividly his calling on Damascus Road.

It's always great to obey God, as we never know

what He's preparing us for. Around the year 2018, the Lord put in my heart to read the New Testament a lot but focus more on the epistles written by Apostle Paul. I watched many movies about him and studied him like never before. I began to appreciate his calling and why he suffered for Christ's sake. Apostle Paul was never physically part of Jesus's disciples, but He did even more than those physically present with Jesus.

After I finished my first book, *"Intimacy with Christ Jesus,"* the Lord immediately gave me this second assignment. The topic was SPOT-ON, but I began asking Him questions. He kept confirming by making me see the word CHOSEN on every medium. For instance, I will check my emails, and a sale or advertisement from a store specifically says CHOSEN for you. I will turn on the TV to TBN or Daystar, and they will discuss God's CHOSEN, the CHOSEN disciples, or why we are the CHOSEN of Christ. Even when I watch CNN, sometimes, as soon as I tune in, I hear them say someone has been chosen for a particular appointment. This continues till today, and I knew that this was my assignment. Gradually, God brought it all together, but I struggled to find time to write and put it together. I was given this specific assignment in 2022, and fast forward to April 2024. I am now writing this chapter and focusing more because the Lord will not let me rest until this is completed.

I am not going to be partial and say this is my favorite chapter, but I am excited to share with you why it is no coincidence that Christ chose Apostle Paul and why He suffered for the sake of Christ. When you have a calling of God upon your life, and God has chosen you to do exploits for His sake, trust me, nothing will come easy. The Lord will be with you, but you will endure persecution, trials, and rejection from all quarters. Your testimony will be powerful and complete when you can persevere and trust solely in the God who has called you to be with you and guide you.

Apostle Paul, originally known as Saul of Tarsus, was a prominent figure in early Christianity. Born into a Jewish family and raised as a Pharisee, he initially persecuted Christians, believing them to be a threat to Judaism. His dramatic conversion occurred on the road to Damascus, where he experienced a blinding vision of Jesus. This pivotal moment marked the beginning of his mission to spread the Gospel.

God chose Paul as an apostle to the Gentiles, reflecting a divine plan to expand the Christian message beyond the Jewish community. His extensive travels throughout the Roman Empire facilitated the establishment of numerous churches, and he authored many of the New Testament letters, addressing theological issues and providing guidance to early Christians.

Despite his fervent dedication, Paul faced significant suffering for his faith. He endured imprisonment, beatings, shipwrecks, and constant danger from both authorities and hostile communities. His writings often emphasize the theme of suffering as part of the Christian experience, portraying it as a means of sharing in Christ's sufferings and ultimately leading to spiritual growth and deeper faith.

Paul's life and ministry exemplify the transformative power of grace, the importance of perseverance in the face of adversity, and the universal call to share Christ's message with all people.

The story of Apostle Paul is one of transformation, determination, and unwavering faith. From a fervent persecutor of Christians to one of the most influential apostles in Christian history, Paul's life sums up the essence of God's grace and the call to serve. This chapter will explore Paul's calling, the reasons behind his selection as a key figure in early Christianity, the profound suffering he endured for his faith, and why he is often classified as the foremost apostle.

Paul's journey begins with a dramatic encounter on the road to Damascus. Initially known as Saul, he was a zealous Pharisee who believed he was protecting Judaism by persecuting Christians. His fervor led him to hunt down followers of Christ, imprisoning many and even overseeing executions. However, this zealousness was about to be radically transformed.

On his way to Damascus, Saul experienced a blinding light and heard the voice of Jesus asking, *"Saul, why are you persecuting me?" (Acts 9:4)*. This moment marked the turning point in his life and when God chose him. After three days of blindness, he was healed by Ananias, a disciple chosen by God. This profound experience not only led to Saul's conversion but also set him on a new trajectory. He became Paul, an apostle commissioned and chosen to spread the Gospel to the Gentiles.

Paul's calling was significant for several reasons. Firstly, he was uniquely positioned as a Roman citizen with a deep knowledge of Jewish law and culture, allowing him to bridge the gap between Jewish and Gentile audiences. Secondly, his transformation from persecutor to preacher was a powerful testimony of God's mercy and grace, illustrating that no one is beyond redemption.

Paul's commitment to his calling came at a high cost. Throughout his ministry, he faced relentless challenges and persecution. His travels took him across the Roman Empire, where he established churches and preached the Gospel. However, he also encountered opposition that resulted in severe hardships.

In 2 Corinthians 11:24-27, Paul recounts his sufferings: *"Five times I received at the hands of the Jews the forty lashes less one. Three times I was beaten with rods. Once I was stoned. Three times I was shipwrecked; a night and a day I was adrift at sea."* He faced imprisonment, was frequently in danger from both his own people and Gentiles and endured physical and emotional pain.

Yet, amid suffering, Paul found strength and purpose. His letters often reflect a deep understanding of suffering as part of the Christian experience, teaching that trials can lead to spiritual growth and a closer relationship with Christ. He famously wrote in Philippians 3:10 that he desired to *"know Christ and the power of his resurrection, and the fellowship of sharing in his sufferings."*

Paul's designation as the foremost apostle in the early church can be attributed to several factors. First, his extensive missionary journeys and the establishment of numerous churches across diverse regions greatly expanded the reach of Christianity. Unlike the other apostles whose ministries were primarily centered in Judea, Paul's work spanned the Mediterranean, making the message of Christ accessible to Gentiles.

Paul's theological contributions to Christianity are immense. His letters, which comprise a significant portion of the New Testament, address essential doctrines, ethics, and the nature of the church. His teachings on grace, faith, and the role of the Holy Spirit have shaped Christian theology and continue to influence believers today.

Despite immense suffering, Paul's unwavering commitment to his mission exemplifies a remarkable dedication to Christ. His life is a model for perseverance in faith, inspiring countless Christians throughout history to embrace their callings and endure hardships for the sake of the Gospel.

The Apostle Paul stands as a towering figure in Christianity, not merely for his prolific writings but for the radical transformation he underwent and his relentless dedication to spreading the message of Christ. His calling, marked by a divine encounter, propelled him into a life of service fraught with suffering yet filled with purpose. As the foremost apostle, Paul's legacy continues to resonate, reminding believers of the power of grace, the importance of perseverance, and the call to share the Gospel with all nations. His life is a testament to the transformative power of faith and the enduring impact one individual can have in advancing the cause of Christ.

Apostle Paul's letters, known as epistles, contain several common themes that reflect his theological insights, pastoral concerns, and practical advice for early Christians.

Paul emphasizes salvation by grace through faith, highlighting that it is not by works but a gift from God *(Ephesians 2:8-9)*. He often contrasts grace with the law, explaining how faith in Christ fulfills the requirements of the law.

A central theme in Paul's letters is the person and work of Jesus Christ. He discusses Christ's divinity, humanity, death, and resurrection, presenting Jesus as the cornerstone of faith and the fulfillment of God's promises *(Philippians 2:5-11)*.

Paul frequently describes the church as the body of Christ, emphasizing the unity and diversity of believers. He encourages the use of spiritual gifts for the edification of the church and stresses the importance of community and mutual support *(1 Corinthians 12)*.

Paul explores the concept of justification, explaining that believers are made righteous before God through faith in Christ *(Romans 5:1)*. He discusses the implications of being justified, including the transformation of life and the call to live righteously.

The role of the Holy Spirit is a recurring theme, where Paul highlights the Spirit's work in the believer's life, including empowerment for service, guidance, and the production of spiritual fruit *(Galatians 5:22-23)*.

Paul addresses the reality of suffering in the Christian life, encouraging believers to find hope and strength in their trials. He often relates suffering to sharing in Christ's sufferings and the eventual glory that awaits believers *(Romans 8:17)*.

Many of Paul's letters touch on eschatological themes, including the return of Christ, the resurrection of the dead, and the hope of eternal life. He encourages believers to remain steadfast in their faith in light of future promises *(1 Thessalonians 4:13-18)*.

Paul emphasizes the importance of love as the greatest commandment and the foundation of Christian relationships. He often calls for unity among believers, urging them to resolve conflicts and work together for the common good *(1 Corinthians 13; Ephesians 4:1-3)*.

Paul provides practical instructions on how

Christians should live, emphasizing moral integrity, ethical behavior, and the importance of living in a manner worthy of their calling *(Colossians 3:1-17)*.

Paul's letters reflect his commitment to spreading the Gospel. He encourages believers to share their faith and be active in the mission of the church, demonstrating the importance of evangelism in the life of a Christian *(Romans 10:14-15)*.

Paul was chosen to suffer for Christ as part of a broader divine plan. In Acts 9:15-16, God tells Ananias that Paul is a *"chosen instrument"* to proclaim His name to the Gentiles and that he will suffer greatly for the sake of the Gospel. This suffering was not ordinary but a means to fulfill God's purpose in spreading Christianity.

Paul's suffering allowed him to identify closely with Christ's sufferings. In Philippians 3:10, Paul expresses his desire to "know Christ and the power of his resurrection, and the fellowship of sharing in his sufferings." By enduring hardship, he participated in Christ's redemptive suffering, which deepened his relationship with Him.

Paul's sufferings served as a powerful testimony to others about the transformative power of faith. His endurance in the face of persecution demonstrated an unwavering commitment to Christ, encouraging fellow believers to remain steadfast in their own faith despite challenges.

Suffering was also a means of spiritual growth for Paul. He often wrote about how trials refined his character and produced perseverance *(Romans 5:3-5)*. Through his suffering, Paul became more reliant on God's strength and grace, exemplifying that adversity can lead to deeper faith and maturity.

Paul's suffering was linked to his missionary work. He faced opposition and persecution as he traveled to various regions to preach the Gospel. His willingness to suffer for Christ's sake illustrated the urgency and importance of his mission to bring the message of salvation to all people.

The Apostle Paul was chosen to suffer for Christ's sake as part of God's divine plan to spread the Gospel. His sufferings served multiple purposes, including fulfilling his mission, identifying with Christ, providing a testimony of faith, fostering spiritual growth, and exemplifying the call to serve and endure for the sake of others.

Paul was born a Jew but also held Roman citizenship, giving him a unique position to bridge the gap between Jewish and Gentile cultures. His training as a Pharisee provided him with a deep understanding of Jewish law and Scriptures, while his Roman citizenship allowed him to navigate the broader Greco-Roman world effectively. This dual heritage equipped him to articulate Christ's message in a way relevant to Jews and Gentiles.

Paul understood that the Gospel was intended for all people, not just the Jews. His letters frequently emphasize the inclusion of Gentiles in God's redemptive plan, arguing that faith in Christ transcends ethnic and cultural boundaries *(Galatians 3:28)*. He articulated the vision of a universal church where all believers, regardless of background, are united in Christ.

After his conversion, Paul exhibited an extraordinary passion for evangelism. His tireless missionary journeys across the Roman Empire demonstrated his commitment to spreading the Gospel to Gentiles. He established numerous churches and engaged with diverse communities, making him a pivotal figure in the early church's expansion.

Paul articulated profound theological insights about grace, salvation, and the nature of faith that resonated with Gentile audiences. His teachings emphasized that salvation is available to all through faith in Jesus Christ, independent of adherence to the Jewish law *(Ephesians 2:8-9)*. This message was particularly appealing to Gentiles who sought a relationship with God without the burdens of legalistic requirements.

Paul's willingness to suffer for the sake of the Gospel further exemplified his commitment. His hardships and perseverance in the face of persecution were a powerful testimony to Gentiles about the transformative power of faith.

Apostle Paul was chosen to bring salvation to the Gentiles due to his divine calling, unique background, understanding of God's universal plan, missionary zeal, theological insights, and willingness to suffer for the Gospel. His ministry played a crucial role in establishing Christianity as a faith for all people, not limited by ethnicity or cultural background.

Acts 9:1-31 (KJV) "And Saul, yet breathing out threatenings and slaughter against the disciples of the Lord, went unto the high priest,

² And desired of him letters to Damascus to the synagogues, that if he found any of this way, whether they were men or women, he might bring them bound unto Jerusalem.

³ And as he journeyed, he came near Damascus: and suddenly there shined round about him a light from heaven:

⁴ And he fell to the earth, and heard a voice saying unto him, Saul, Saul, why persecutest thou me?

⁵ And he said, Who art thou, Lord? And the Lord said, I am Jesus whom thou persecutest: it is hard for thee to kick against the pricks.

⁶ And he trembling and astonished said, Lord, what wilt thou have me to do? And the Lord said unto him, Arise, and go into the city, and it shall be told thee what thou must do.

⁷ And the men which journeyed with him stood speechless, hearing a voice, but seeing no man.

⁸ And Saul arose from the earth; and when his eyes were opened, he saw no man: but they led him by the hand and brought him into Damascus.

⁹ And he was three days without sight, and neither did eat nor drink.

¹⁰ And there was a certain disciple at Damascus, named Ananias; and to him said the Lord in a vision, Ananias. And he said, Behold, I am here, Lord.

¹¹ And the Lord said unto him, Arise, and go into the street, which is called Straight, and enquire in the house of Judas for one called Saul, of Tarsus: for, behold, he prayeth,

¹² And hath seen in a vision a man named Ananias

coming in, and putting his hand on him, that he might receive his sight.

¹³ Then Ananias answered, Lord, I have heard by many of this man, how much evil he hath done to thy saints at Jerusalem:

¹⁴ And here he hath authority from the chief priests to bind all that call on thy name.

¹⁵ But the Lord said unto him, Go thy way: for he is a chosen vessel unto me, to bear my name before the Gentiles, and kings, and the children of Israel:

¹⁶ For I will shew him how great things he must suffer for my name's sake.

¹⁷ And Ananias went his way and entered into the house; and putting his hands on him said, Brother Saul, the Lord, even Jesus, that appeared unto thee in the way as thou camest, hath sent me, that thou mightest receive thy sight, and be filled with the Holy Ghost.

¹⁸ And immediately there fell from his eyes as it had been scales: and he received sight forthwith, and arose, and was baptized.

¹⁹ And when he had received meat, he was strengthened. Then was Saul certain days with the disciples which were at Damascus.

²⁰ And straightway he preached Christ in the

synagogues, that he is the Son of God.

²¹ But all that heard him were amazed, and said; Is not this he that destroyed them which called on this name in Jerusalem, and came hither for that intent, that he might bring them bound unto the chief priests?

²² But Saul increased the more in strength, and confounded the Jews which dwelt at Damascus, proving that this is very Christ.

²³ And after that many days were fulfilled, the Jews took counsel to kill him:

²⁴ But their laying await was known of Saul. And they watched the gates day and night to kill him.

²⁵ Then the disciples took him by night and let him down by the wall in a basket.

²⁶ And when Saul was come to Jerusalem, he assayed to join himself to the disciples: but they were all afraid of him, and believed not that he was a disciple.

²⁷ But Barnabas took him, and brought him to the apostles, and declared unto them how he had seen the Lord in the way, and that he had spoken to him, and how he had preached boldly at Damascus in the name of Jesus.

²⁸ And he was with them coming in and going out

at Jerusalem.

²⁹ And he spake boldly in the name of the Lord Jesus, and disputed against the Grecians: but they went about to slay him.

³⁰ Which when the brethren knew, they brought him down to Caesarea and sent him forth to Tarsus.

³¹ Then had the churches rest throughout all Judaea and Galilee and Samaria, and were edified; and walking in the fear of the Lord, and in the comfort of the Holy Ghost, were multiplied.

As he traveled and was nearing Damascus, a light from heaven suddenly flashed around him. Falling to the ground, he heard a voice saying to him, *"Saul, Saul, why are you persecuting me?" "Who are you, Lord?"* Saul said. *"I am Jesus, the one you are persecuting,"* He replied. *"But get up and go into the city, and you will be told what you must do."*

God only gives us the next step, not the whole plan. When Jesus spoke to Paul, He didn't say, hey Saul, you're going to go to a man's house for a few days, then meet one of my disciples who will restore your sight. After that, you're going to hang out with my disciples to learn more about me, then go on several huge missions to tell others about me. And then you're going to write a bunch of letters to a bunch of churches, then finally, you'll be beheaded, dying as a martyr for the kingdom of God."

Can you imagine how bizarre and overwhelming that would have sounded? Instead, Jesus said, *"But get up and go into the city, and you will be told what you must do."* God requires faith. We must trust Him completely, sometimes taking blind steps, as Paul did, toward the unknown. We must trust that God has everything under control and will reveal the next step when we need it.

God uses imperfect people to do His perfect work. Repeatedly in scripture, we meet ordinary or even extraordinarily bad people who are the most unlikely candidates for God to use for His kingdom.

But time and again, we see God doing just that, just like He used Paul. Paul went from persecutor of Christians to the greatest apostle of all time. The death of Jesus washes away ALL sin for ALL people, not just some sin for some people. We may think we are beyond saving, or we've done too many bad things in our lives for God to love us and use us for His kingdom, but we are wrong. There is no sin too big that the blood of Jesus can't cover. As finite men, we have our limitations and we cannot comprehend the ways of the infinite

God. However, we should not use this as an excuse for our neglect and failure. God desires us to grow in our understanding of Him and His ways so that we can have quality fellowship with Him and participate more meaningfully and effectively in His purposes.

God desires to teach us and reveal to us much through His Spirit. Therefore, we must seek Him earnestly, diligently, and humbly. This is an essential aspect of our friendship with God. One major reason we fail to understand people and situations accurately is our failure to perceive reality beyond their outward appearance.

1 Timothy 1:12-15 *[12] I thank Christ Jesus our Lord, who has strengthened me, because He considered me faithful, putting me into service, [13] even though I was formerly a blasphemer and a persecutor and a violent aggressor. Yet I was shown mercy because I acted ignorantly in unbelief; [14] and the grace of our Lord was more than abundant, with the faith and love which are found in Christ Jesus. [15] It is a trustworthy statement, deserving full acceptance, that Christ Jesus came into the world to save sinners, among whom I am foremost of all.*

The state of a person's heart before his conversion has a bearing on the quality of his faith and whether he becomes a man of faith. The depth of a person's response and commitment to the Lord at conversion can give him a good start on the road to becoming a man of faith.

"Hardened people" may be near the kingdom of God. Those who appear hardened and antagonistic towards Christians and the Christian faith may not necessarily be far from God's kingdom. Like Paul, some of them, while at the height of their anti-Christian stance, could, in fact, be near to God's kingdom. But it is also true that many who are antagonistic may actually be very far from God's kingdom. When we encounter such situations, we should try to understand the reality and not be deterred by wrong conclusions based on outward appearance.

A person's true state may not be easy to perceive. This is especially true when outward appearance portrays a very different picture from the realities within the heart. Many things that are not obvious may be going on in the person's heart and mind. We need to be alert and open to this possibility instead of being overconfident in our assessment of things and thus concluding hastily. Sometimes, even the person himself may not understand what is going on.

The difficulty in understanding these things can

be illustrated by the initial response of the disciple Ananias to the Lord's instructions to him concerning Paul. The positive impact of Christians may not be noticeable. The conduct and testimony of Christians, including Stephen and others whom Paul had persecuted or observed, might not have positively impacted him. In fact, they infuriated him and caused him to be even more antagonistic. They could have caused him to become less certain about his stand against the Christian faith, thus preparing him for conversion.

In our desire to be faithful witnesses for God when he chooses us, we may sometimes not appear to impact others positively, or we may even appear to infuriate them. Let us not conclude that just because there seems to be no positive impact, there is indeed none. However, we need to exercise care so that our lives and conduct do not hinder others from entering the kingdom of God.

Generally, a person's conversion is not solely due to a particular experience or event. Many things would have been taking place in his life. It is an ongoing process, and along the way, the testimonies of faithful brethren would have contributed to the final positive outcome.

Believers can also significantly contribute to the

quality of conversion response through their faithful lives and words. The likelihood of a quality conversion is higher if the testimony is strong. After becoming a Christian, a person can often look back and point to the positive impact of Christians he encountered or whose lives he observed, even those observed from a distance.

We should, therefore, not think that our lives have no positive impact on others just because they appear that way. Though a person's response to God is a matter of personal choice, it is nevertheless important that we, as lights of the world, strive to be faithful to God because, potentially, the impact on others can be very significant.

In the same way, we should not conclude that our lives significantly impact others just because it appears to be that way. They may be merely expressing superficial words, sometimes out of politeness, without a deep response from the heart.

Faithful testimony of Christians can positively impact others not only at conversion but also after conversion. After conversion, a person can still reflect on the quality of the testimony he had observed in the lives of believers. This can be a source of encouragement for him and can contribute significantly to his spiritual development even long after the event. However, if there is little quality, the impact is likely to be minimal. For example, it is unlikely that Paul would forget the life and testimony of Stephen and the other faithful disciples and their willingness to suffer for the Lord. They would have encouraged him to be earnest and faithful and helped prepare him for a life of suffering for the faith.

God knew from the beginning that the ministry He chose for Paul would include much suffering. God told Ananias in Acts 9:15-16 that Paul was not only a *"chosen instrument"* of God but also one who would suffer much for His name's sake.

In later years, Paul wrote much about the place and meaningfulness of suffering in Christian living. In Philippians 1:29, Paul expresses that suffering is a privilege: "For to you it has been granted for Christ's sake, not only to believe in Him but also to suffer for His sake". He teaches that suffering for the Lord's sake can be a very meaningful experience for faithful Christians. Philippians 3:10 says that I may know Him and the power of His resurrection and the fellowship of His sufferings, being conformed to His death. Colossians 1:24 Now I rejoice in my sufferings for your sake, and in my flesh, I do my share on behalf of His body, which is the church, in filling up what is lacking in Christ's afflictions.

In his epistle to the Corinthians, he elaborates on the principle of suffering and death and how it produces life in others:

2 Corinthians 4:8-12 8 We are afflicted in every way, but not crushed; perplexed, but not despairing; 9 persecuted, but not forsaken; struck down, but not destroyed; 10 always carrying about in the body the dying of Jesus, so that the life of Jesus also may be manifested in our body 11 For we who live are constantly being delivered over to death for Jesus' sake, so that the life of Jesus also may be manifested in our mortal flesh. 12 So death works in us, but life in you.

It is possible that Paul learned to appreciate the meaning and purpose of suffering in a Christian's life through his personal experience and by observing and being encouraged by Stephen and the other believers' positive example.

The true man of faith will persevere and run the race well until he finishes his course on earth. Paul's life and faithful ministry from his conversion to the end of his time on earth is a good illustration of this point and a powerful testimony to how much God can do in and through a man of faith.

In this chapter, we have sought to understand

Paul's conversion and calling as an apostle. These events in his life may seem sudden and incomprehensible because he was a violent and relentless persecutor of the church just before his conversion. Yet, as we have examined, Paul was seeking zealously to serve God and keep His laws. The Lord saw beyond Paul's apparent anti-God and anti-Christian stance. He knew Paul's actual state of heart and the positive qualities within him. This helps us understand the Lord's intervention in Paul's life, which led to his conversion and calling as an apostle. Paul vindicated God's confidence in him as God's chosen. The moment he was converted, he became a committed disciple of the Lord. He labored hard to serve the Lord and did not receive the grace of God in vain. Paul became an outstanding example of a man of faith.

We learn from this that what motivates our outward conduct is more important than the outward conduct itself. Ultimately, God is most concerned about what lies within our hearts. However, let us not give excuses for our improper conduct by saying, *"My heart's attitudes are right; outward conduct does not matter."* Although appearance does not always reflect reality, our outward conduct often flows forth from what is within the heart and reveals its true state. It can help us understand ourselves and others.

The faithful testimony of the disciples of Christ in the face of fiery persecution would likely have had a positive impact on the life of Paul, even though outwardly he continued to persecute Christians. It would have stirred Paul's heart and helped to prepare him to receive the Lord Jesus. It would also have contributed much to Paul's faithful ministry as an apostle in the years that followed.

Let us not be deterred by outward appearance but learn to persevere in faithful service and witness to the truth. There are those who may appear to be hardened towards the truth but, in reality, are near God's kingdom. If we live well, we can significantly impact others, even though it may not appear so. Let us take courage and not lose heart. The more wholeheartedly we live for the Lord, the more significant the impact of our lives in the spiritual realm.

God desires to do a deep work in our lives so that we can bear much fruit. Like Paul, let us fully submit to God and learn to strive according to His power and guidance.

Paul describes his specific calling in the book of Romans. *"Paul, a servant of Christ Jesus, called to be an apostle, set apart for the gospel of God…" (Romans*

1:1). Paul's calling to be *"set apart"* for the gospel defined him from the moment that it took place.

Apostle Paul is traditionally believed to have written the following books in the New Testament: *Romans, 1 Corinthians, 2 Corinthians, Galatians, Ephesians, Philippians, Colossians, 1 Thessalonians, 2 Thessalonians, 1 Timothy, 2 Timothy, Titus and Philemon.*

These letters, also known as epistles, were written by Paul to various churches and individuals during his missionary journeys. They address theological, ethical, and practical issues faced by the early Christian communities.

Firstly, Paul was a highly educated and zealous Pharisee who was deeply committed to his Jewish faith. His background and knowledge of Jewish law made him uniquely qualified to bridge the gap between Jewish and Gentile believers in the early Christian community.

Secondly, Paul's conversion experience on the road to Damascus, where he encountered the risen Jesus Christ, was transformative. This encounter led to his conversion to Christianity and his subsequent mission to spread the Gospel to the Gentiles as God's chosen.

Lastly, Paul's passion, dedication, and perseverance in spreading the message of Christ, despite facing numerous hardships and persecution, demonstrated his unwavering commitment to his calling. His writings and teachings have profoundly impacted the development of Christian theology and the spread of Christianity worldwide.

Paul's unique combination of background, experience, and unwavering commitment to the Gospel made him a chosen and powerful instrument in God's plan to spread the message of salvation to all people.

In summary, the Apostle Paul's encounter with the risen Jesus Christ on the road to Damascus transformed his life. It led to his conversion to Christianity and completely redirected his mission. It propelled him to become one of the most influential chosen figures in the early Christian church, spreading Christ's message to Jews and Gentiles.

As an Apostle and missionary chosen by Christ, Paul faced various forms of persecution throughout his ministry. His commitment to spreading the Gospel and bold teachings led to opposition and hostility from Jewish leaders and Gentile authorities. Here are some examples of the persecution that Paul endured.

Paul faced significant opposition from Jewish religious leaders who saw him as a threat to their traditional beliefs and practices. They often stirred up crowds against him, accusing him of blasphemy and heresy. Paul was frequently arrested, beaten, and imprisoned by Jewish authorities.

Paul endured multiple imprisonments throughout his ministry. He was imprisoned in Philippi, Thessalonica, and ultimately in Rome. Harsh conditions and mistreatment often accompanied these imprisonments.

Paul experienced severe physical beatings on several occasions. In one instance, he was stoned and left for dead in Lystra. He also mentions being beaten with rods on multiple occasions.

Paul faced constant threats in his life from those who opposed his message. In many cities, there were plots to kill him. He had to escape from Damascus by being lowered in a basket through an opening in the city wall, and he faced numerous other escape attempts.

While traveling, Paul endured numerous hardships, including shipwrecks, being adrift at sea, and exposure to the elements. These experiences were often life-threatening.

Despite the persecution and hardships, Paul remained steadfast in his faith and commitment to spreading the Gospel. He saw these challenges as opportunities to testify to the power of Christ and his message of salvation. Paul's perseverance and unwavering devotion to his mission inspire Christians today.

| CHAPTER 4 |

WHY THE CHOSEN SUFFER PERSECUTION

Every serious Born-Again Believer and Christian I know, including myself, have asked the question at some point in their life, "Why am I going through this, Lord? What are you doing?" What you thought God was supposed to do, He did not do. When you thought God would show up, it seemed He did not. And it left you confused, shattered, disappointed, frustrated, rebellious, upset, and maybe even doubting God altogether.

In times like this, many Christians like me begin to question God. "God, if you are supposedly working in my life, why aren't you answering me? Why does it seem things are not going how I want them to?" The problem with those thoughts is that we assume that being chosen by God means being selected for comfort, a struggle-free life filled with perfection and success. But often, being chosen leads to opposition, discomfort, and hardship.

If you have placed your faith in Christ, be rest assured that God chose you. Believe that God is working something mighty in you when life is hard. When life seems unfair, believe that God is preparing you. You have got to cling to the promise that God will be faithful to you as He was to Paul. So, when suffering comes, you can declare with Paul, *"I will boast all the more gladly of my weaknesses so that the power of Christ may rest upon me. For the sake of Christ, then, I am content with weaknesses, insults, hardships, persecutions, and calamities. For when I am weak, then I am strong." (2 Corinthians 12:9)*

Psalm 129

A song of ascents.
[1] *"They have greatly oppressed me from my youth,"*
 let Israel say;
[2] *"they have greatly oppressed me from my youth,*
 but they have not gained the victory over me.
[3] *Plowmen have plowed my back*
 and made their furrows long.

⁴ But the Lord is righteous;
   he has cut me free from the cords of the wicked."
⁵ May all who hate Zion
   be turned back in shame.
⁶ May they be like grass on the roof,
   which withers before it can grow;
⁷ a reaper cannot fill his hands with it,
   nor one who gathers fill his arms.
⁸ May those who pass by not say to them,
   "The blessing of the Lord be on you;
   we bless you in the name of the Lord

Christians, as we know, are not exempt from suffering, particularly the persecution that arises from identifying with Christ. While our trials may vary in nature, every Christian will experience some degree of suffering. It could manifest as insults, disparaging remarks, struggles with sin, disappointments in a broken world, tragic losses, poverty, imprisonment, rejection, betrayal, disappointments, or even death. Early Christians endured intense persecution, and many struggled with discouragement. Peter's encouragement went beyond superficial motivation to ease their pain as it offered a hope that transcended their temporary discomfort.

    Modern Christians often hold one of two extreme

views of suffering. The first extreme treats suffering as either an illusion or a sign of weak faith. This perspective suggests that Christians should not suffer, and even mentioning negative aspects of life, like sickness, is almost sinful. The books of Job and Ecclesiastes refute this view, and in the New Testament, Jesus affirms that His followers will face trials and persecution (Matthew 5:10–12; Luke 9:23; John 16:33). Even Hebrews 11, the renowned chapter on faith, acknowledges suffering (verses 35–38). The other extreme involves adopting a defeatist attitude toward life due to its brokenness. Both extremes should be avoided, considering God's promises.

God's first encouragement to Christians, through Peter, is restoration. The word "restore" conveys the idea of making something whole again. Sin and suffering have left us broken, and we will not be fully restored on this side of eternity. However, at the right time, God will restore all things. From a Christian perspective, the afterlife is not just a consolation for the troubles of the present life but a renewal of God's intended state.

Additionally, God promises to confirm, strengthen, and establish us. He fully acknowledges that we are His, that He gifts us with strength, and that He will establish us; that is, He will keep us rooted. Through it all, *"our light and momentary troubles are achieving for us an eternal glory that far outweighs them all" (2 Corinthians 4:17).*

Hence, we need not deny the reality of suffering for the righteous individuals or those who fall into despair. It can be dismaying to witness the prevalence of evil in the world, and we may wonder why God appears silent. However, the God who suffered in the Person of Jesus has shown us that He is active both in good and bad times. We can always rely on His grace when the burden feels too much to bear.

Most of the time, people who are chosen by God have gone through a lot, and they have so many stories to share. They have been rejected, gone through persecution, afflictions, shame, disappointments, disgrace, reproach, lied upon and betrayed. There is no doubt that persecution is a stark reality of living the Christian life. Christian persecution is to be expected as the Apostle Paul warned that *"everyone who wants to live a godly life in Christ Jesus will be persecuted" (2 Timothy 3:12).* Jesus said that if they persecuted Him, they will also persecute His followers *(John 15:20).* Jesus made it clear that those of the world will hate Christians because the world hates Christ. If Christians were like the world who are vain, earthly, sensual, and given to pleasure, wealth, and ambition, then the world would not oppose us.

But Christians do not belong to the world, which is why the world engages in Christian persecution *(John 15:18–19)*. Christians are influenced by different principles from those of the world. We are motivated by the love of God and holiness, while the love of sin drives the world. Our very separation from the world arouses the world's animosity *(1 Peter 4:3–4)*.

Christians must learn to recognize the value of persecution and even to rejoice in it, not in a conspicuous way but quietly and humbly, because persecution has great spiritual value. First, the persecution of Christians allows them to share in a unique fellowship with the Lord. Paul outlined several things he had surrendered for the cause of Christ. Such losses, however, he viewed as "rubbish" *(Philippians 3:8)* or "dung" (KJV) that he might share in the *"fellowship of [Christ's] sufferings" (Philippians 3:10)*. The noble apostle even counted his chains as a grace that God had bestowed upon him *(Philippians 1:7)*.

In all truth, Christian persecution is good for believers. James argues that trials test the Christian's faith, develop endurance in his life, and help develop maturity *(James 1:2–4)*. As steel is tempered in the forge, trials and persecution, serve to strengthen the character of believers. A Christian yielding graciously to persecution demonstrates that he is of superior quality as compared to his adversaries *(see Hebrews 11:38)*. It's easy to be hateful, but Christlikeness produces kindness and blessing in the face of evil opposition. Peter says of Jesus, *"When they hurled their insults at Him, He did not retaliate; when He suffered, He made no threats. Instead, He entrusted Himself to Him who judges justly" (1 Peter 2:23).*

    Christian persecution enables believers to better value the support of true friends. Conflict can bring faithful children of God together in an encouraging and supportive way they might not have known otherwise. Hardship can stimulate the Lord's people toward a greater resolve to love and comfort one another and lift one another to the throne of grace in prayer. There's nothing like an unpleasant incident to help us reach a greater level of brotherly love.

    Even in the face of Christian persecution, we can press on. We can thank God for His grace and patience with us. We can express gratitude to those whom we love in the Lord and who stand with us in times of distress. And we can pray for those who would accuse, misuse, or abuse us *(2 Corinthians 11:24; Romans*

10:1).

The Chosen are the ones who have faced challenges and are now deemed worthy and qualified. All around the world, intolerance and persecution of Christians are increasing. And even though we may face discrimination or judgment, the reality for many of us in the West is that we will never experience similar violence or oppression. Yet persecution has been a part of Christianity's story since its beginning in Acts 4 & 5. It's an uncomfortable thought but an important one. At some point or other, we may find ourselves grappling with whether persecution is worth it. In such moments, remember what Jesus promised: *"Theirs is the kingdom of heaven" (Matthew 5:10)*. He wasn't being intentionally vague as He was talking specifically about us, His followers. As Christians, we simply won't experience the fullness of life if we're not willing to risk loving Him above all else, even if it costs us our job, our place in society, or our very life.

Peter encourages his readers to be ready to suffer for righteousness. He tells them that even if their persecution results in sacrificing their lives as Christ did, God, their judge, will honor and reward them in heaven. Peter commands them to arm themselves by adopting the attitude of Christ. Christ suffered not for doing what was wrong but for doing what was right. As a result, His crucifixion freed us from the power of sin. With this incredible burden lifted, we can now concentrate on following Christ's will for our lives rather than our own needs. As we build momentum in conquering sin, we become more spiritually mature.

Being chosen by God does not mean that a person will always enjoy his life and he will have authority over others. The real fact is that God molds the person whom he calls for his work. God called Abraham and made him deny his family and country to concentrate on his mission. He taught him that he must stick to him so he will have the mindset to work for his mission.

Joseph was called by the Lord to prepare the scene for his people's lives under the bondage of the Pharaohs. He was to seek God while he was separated from his brothers and father and placed in the house of Potiphar. Later, he was sent to jail. But the Lord blessed him and used him mightily despite his many trials.

Even Abraham also had experienced many tests in his life to be worthy of being chosen. The Lord kept him fatherless until he reached his old age, and he found that he would die without a son, but God blessed him by making him the father of the nation Israel through his son Issac. Moses also was chosen by the Lord, and he suffered in his life due to the calling of God, yet he was blessed. God did many miraculous works through him and made him known that He could select anyone worthy of his specific works.

When God chooses us, we go through Trials, Transformation and Triumphs. One of the most challenging parts of the Christian life is the fact that becoming a disciple of Christ does not make us immune to life's trials and tribulations. Why would a good and loving God allow us to go through such things as the death of a child, disease, and injury to ourselves and our loved ones, financial hardships, worry, and fear? Indeed, if He loved us, He would take all these things away from us. After all, doesn't loving us mean He wants our lives to be easy and comfortable? Well, no, it doesn't. The Bible teaches that God loves those who are His children, and He *"works all things together for good" for us (Romans 8:28).* That must mean that the trials and tribulations He allows in our lives are part of the working together of all things for good. Therefore, for the believer, all trials and tribulations must have a divine purpose.

As in all things, God's ultimate purpose for us is to grow more and more into the image of His Son *(Romans 8:29).* This is the goal of the Christian, and everything in life, including the trials and tribulations, is designed to enable us to reach that goal. It is part of the process of sanctification, being set apart for God's purposes and fitted to live for His glory. The way trials accomplish this is explained in 1 Peter 1:6-7: *"In this you greatly rejoice, even though now for a little while, if necessary, you have been distressed by various trials, that the proof of your faith, being more precious than gold which perishes, even though tested by fire, may be found to result in praise and glory and honor at the revelation of Jesus Christ."* The true believer's faith will be made sure by the trials we experience so that we can rest in the knowledge that it is real and will last forever.

Trials develop godly character, and that enables us to *"rejoice in our sufferings, because we know that suffering produces perseverance; perseverance, character; and character, hope. And hope does not disappoint us, because God has poured out his love into our hearts by the Holy Spirit, whom he has given us"* *(Romans 5:3-5)*. Jesus Christ set the perfect example. *"But God demonstrates His own love toward us, in that while we were yet sinners, Christ died for us" (Romans 5:8)*. These verses reveal aspects of His divine purpose for both Jesus Christ's trials and tribulations and ours.

Persevering proves our faith. *"I can do all things through Christ, who strengthens me" (Philippians 4:13).*

However, we must be careful never to make excuses for our "trials and tribulations" if they are a result of our own wrongdoing. *"By no means let any of you suffer as a murderer, or thief, or evildoer, or a troublesome meddler" (1 Peter 4:15).* God will forgive our sins because the eternal punishment for them has been paid by Christ's sacrifice on the cross. However, we still must suffer the natural consequences of our sins and bad choices in life. But God uses even those sufferings to mold and shape us for His purposes and our ultimate good.

Trials and tribulations come with both purpose and reward. *"Consider it all joy, my brethren, when you encounter various trials, knowing that the testing of your faith produces endurance. And let endurance have its perfect result, that you may be perfect and complete, lacking in nothing. Blessed is the man who perseveres under trial; for once he has been approved, he will receive the crown of life, which the Lord has promised to those who love Him" (James 1:2-4,12).*

Through all of life's trials and tribulations, we have the victory. *"But thanks be to God, who gives us the victory through our Lord, Jesus Christ."* Although we are in a spiritual battle, Satan has no authority over the believer in Christ. God has given us His Word to guide us, His Holy Spirit to enable us, and the privilege of coming to Him anywhere, at any time, to pray about anything.

I remember when I said, *"Why, God, why this, and why that?"* God told me to wait for His timing. He has delivered me in the past, but when you are going through bad times, all you think about is right now. I've seen God use trials to build me up, answer different prayers, open doors, and help others, and I've seen many miracles where I knew only God could have done this.

While I was worrying, the Lord gave me comfort, encouragement, and motivation, and He was working behind the scenes. If, as believers, we're burdened when our brothers and sisters suffer, imagine how God feels. Always remember that He loves you and reminds us time after time in His Word that He will never forsake us. James 1:12: *"God blesses those who patiently endure testing and temptation. Afterward they will receive the crown of life that God has promised to those who love him."*

Galatians 6:9: *"Let us not become weary in doing*

good, for at the proper time we will reap a harvest if we do not give up." Hebrews 10:35-36 "So do not throw away your confidence; it will be richly rewarded. You need to persevere so that when you have done the will of God, you will receive what he has promised."

Sometimes, we must admit we just don't know, and instead of going crazy and trying to find out why, we must trust in the Lord that He knows best. Isaiah 55:8-9 "For my thoughts are not your thoughts, neither are your ways my ways," declares the Lord. "As the heavens are higher than the earth, so are my ways higher than your ways and my thoughts than your thoughts." Jeremiah 29:11: "For I know the plans I have for you, declares the Lord, plans to prosper you and not to harm you, plans to give you hope and a future." Proverbs 3:5 -6: "Trust in the LORD with all your heart; do not depend on your own understanding. Seek his will in all you do, and he will show you which path to take."

In my life, I've suffered because I have followed the wrong voice. I did my will instead of God's will. I can't blame God for my mistakes, but what I can say is God brought me through it and made me stronger and wiser in the process. Hosea 4:6: *"My people are destroyed from lack of knowledge. "Because you have rejected knowledge, I also reject you as my priests;*

because you have ignored the law of your God, I also will ignore your children." Proverbs 19:2-3 *"Desire without knowledge is not good– how much more will hasty feet miss the way! A person's own folly leads to their ruin, yet their heart rages against the LORD."*

We can suffer because God is making us more humble. 2 Corinthians 12:7: *"Even though I have received such wonderful revelations from God. So, to keep me from becoming proud, I was given a thorn in my flesh, a messenger from Satan to torment me and keep me from becoming proud."* Proverbs 18:12: *"Before destruction a man's heart is haughty, but humility comes before honor."* 1 Peter 5:6-8 *"Humble yourselves, therefore, under God's mighty hand, that he may lift you up in due time. Cast all your anxiety on him because he cares for you. Be alert and of sober mind. Your enemy, the devil prowls around like a roaring lion looking for someone to devour."*

God's discipline can also cause suffering. Hebrews 12:5-11 "And have you completely forgotten this word of encouragement that addresses you as a father addresses his son? It says, *"My son, do not make light of the Lord's discipline, and do not lose heart when he rebukes you, because the Lord disciplines the one he loves, and he chastens everyone he accepts as his son."*

Endure hardship as discipline; God is treating you as his children. For what children are not disciplined by their father? If you are not disciplined—and everyone undergoes discipline—then you are not legitimate, not true sons and daughters at all.

Moreover, we have all had human fathers who disciplined us, and we respected them for it. How much more should we submit to the Father of spirits and live! They disciplined us for a little while as they thought best, but God disciplines us for our good so that we may share in his holiness. No discipline seems pleasant at the time but painful. Later, however, it produces a harvest of righteousness and peace for those who have been trained by it." Proverbs 3:11-13 *"My child, do not reject the Lord's discipline, and don't get angry when he corrects you. The Lord corrects those he loves, just as parents correct the child they delight in. Happy is the person who finds wisdom, the one who gets understanding."*

We can become more dependent on the Lord through trials and suffering. 2 Corinthians 12:9-10 Each time, he said, *"My grace is all you need. My power works best in weakness."* So now I am glad to boast about my weaknesses, so that the power of Christ can work through me. That's why I take pleasure in my weaknesses and the insults, hardships, persecutions, and troubles I suffer for Christ. For when I am weak, then I am strong." John 15:5: *"Yes, I am the vine; you are the branches. Those who remain in me, and I in them, will produce much fruit. For apart from me, you can do nothing."*

God wants to spend time with us, but we lost our first love. You're doing all these things for Jesus, but we're not spending quality quiet time with the Lord. Revelation 2:2-5 *"I know what you do, how you work hard and never give up. I know you do not put up with the false teachings of evil people. You have tested those who say they are apostles but really are not, and you found they are liars. You have patience and have suffered troubles for my name and have not given up. But I have this against you: You have left the love you had in the beginning. So, remember where you were before you fell. Change your hearts and do what you did at first. If you do not change, I will come to you and will take away your lampstand from its place."*

We share in the sufferings of Christ through trials. 1 Peter 4:12-16 *"Dear friends, do not be surprised at the fiery ordeal that has come on you to test you, as though something strange were happening to you. But rejoice inasmuch as you participate in the sufferings of Christ, so that you may be overjoyed when his glory is revealed."* If you are insulted because of the name of Christ, you are blessed, for the Spirit of glory and of God rests on you. If you suffer, it should not be as a murderer or thief or any other kind of criminal or even as a meddler. However, if you suffer as a Christian, do not be ashamed, but praise God that you bear that name. 2 Corinthians 1:5-7 *"For just as we share abundantly in the sufferings of Christ, so also our comfort abounds through Christ. If we are distressed, it is for your comfort and salvation; if we are comforted, it is for your comfort, which produces in you patient endurance of the same sufferings we suffer. And our hope for you is firm because we know that just as you share in our sufferings, so also you share in our comfort."*

Through our trials, we grow as believers and become more like Christ. Romans 8:28-29 *"We know that in everything God works for the good of those who love him. They are the people he called, because that was his plan. God knew them before he made the world, and he chose them to be like his Son so that Jesus would be the firstborn of many brothers and sisters."* Philippians 1:6: *"And I am certain that God, who began the good work within you, will continue his work until it is finally finished on the day when Christ*

Jesus returns." 1 Corinthians 11:1: *"Be imitators of me, as I am of Christ."*

Trials help with developing character. Romans 5:3-6 *"Not only so, but we also glory in our sufferings, because we know that suffering produces perseverance; perseverance, character; and character, hope. And hope does not put us to shame, because God's love has been poured out into our hearts through the Holy Spirit, who has been given to us. You see, at just the right time, when we were still powerless, Christ died for the ungodly."*

Trials help to build our faith in the Lord. James 1:2-6 *"Consider it pure joy, my brothers and sisters, whenever you face trials of many kinds because you know that the testing of your faith produces perseverance. Let perseverance finish its work so that you may be mature and complete, not lacking anything. If any of you lacks wisdom, you should ask God, who gives generously to all without finding fault, and it will be given to you."* Psalm 73:25-28: *"Whom have I in heaven but you? And earth has nothing I desire besides you. My flesh and my heart may fail, but God is the strength of my heart and my portion forever. Those who are far from you will perish; you destroy all who are unfaithful to you. But as for me, it is good to be near God. I have made the Sovereign Lord my refuge; I will tell of all your deeds."*

The storm will not last forever, and trials are an opportunity for a testimony. It gives God so much glory when everyone knows you're going through an arduous trial and you stand strong, trusting in the Lord until He delivers you, without complaining. Psalm 40:4-5 *"Blessed is the one who trusts in the LORD, who does not look to the proud, to those who turn aside to false gods. Many, LORD my God, are the wonders you have done, the things you planned for us. None can compare with you; were I to speak and tell of your deeds, they would be too many to declare."* Psalm 71:14-17 *"As for me, I will always have hope; I will praise you more and more. My mouth will tell of your righteous deeds, of your saving acts all day long— though I know not how to relate them all. I will come and proclaim your mighty acts, Sovereign LORD; I will proclaim your righteous deeds, yours alone."*

You can help someone because you have been in that situation. Throwing around Scriptures will be hard to understand for someone who is grieving, but you can comfort them because you have been through the same thing, and through the pain, you trusted in God. 2 Corinthians 1:3-4 *"Blessed be the God and Father of our Lord Jesus Christ, the Father of mercies and God of all comfort, who comforteth us in all our affliction, that we may be able to comfort them that are in any affliction, through the comfort wherewith we ourselves are comforted of God."* Galatians 6:2: *"Carry each other's burdens, and in this way, you will fulfill the law of Christ."*

Trials give us a greater reward in Heaven. 2 Corinthians 4:16-18: *"Therefore we do not lose heart. Though outwardly we are wasting away, yet inwardly we are being renewed day by day. For our light and momentary troubles are achieving for us an eternal glory that far outweighs them all. So, we fix our eyes not on what is seen, but on what is unseen, since what is seen is temporary, but what is unseen is eternal."* Mark 10:28-30: *"Then Peter spoke up, "We have left everything to follow you!" "Truly I tell you," Jesus replied, "no one who has left home or brothers or sisters or mother or father or children or fields for me and the gospel will fail to receive a hundred times as much in this present age: homes, brothers, sisters, mothers, children, and fields along with persecutions and in the age to come eternal life."*

Trials sometimes show us sin in our lives. We should never deceive ourselves and try to hide our sins from God, which is impossible. Psalm 38:1-11 *"Lord, do not rebuke me in your anger or discipline me in your wrath. Your arrows have pierced me, and your hand has come down on me. Because of your wrath, there is no health in my body; there is no soundness in my bones because of my sin. My guilt has overwhelmed me like a burden too heavy to bear. My wounds fester and are loathsome because of my sinful folly. I am bowed down and brought very low; all day long, I go about mourning. My back is filled with searing pain; there is no health in my body. I am feeble and utterly crushed; I groan in anguish of heart. All my longings lie open before you, Lord; my sighing is not hidden from you. My heart pounds, my strength fails me; even the light has gone from my eyes. My friends and companions avoid me because of my wounds; my neighbors stay far away."* Psalm 38:17-22 *"For I am about to fall, and my pain is ever with me. I confess my iniquity; I am troubled by my sin. Many have become my enemies without cause; those who hate me without reason are numerous. Those who repay my good with evil lodge accusations against me, though I seek only to do what is good. Lord, do not forsake me; do not be far from me, my God. Come quickly to help me, my Lord and my Savior."* Psalm 40:12-13 *"For troubles without number surround me; my sins have overtaken me, and I cannot see. They are more than the hairs of my head, and my heart fails within me. Be pleased to save me, LORD; come quickly, LORD, to help me."*

Trials remind us that it is God who is always in control. Luke 8:22-25 *"One day Jesus said to his disciples, "Let us go over to the other side of the lake."* So, they got into a boat and set out. As they sailed, he fell asleep. A squall came down on the lake, so that the boat was being swamped, and they were in great danger. The disciples went and woke him, saying, "Master, Master, we're going to drown!"* He got up and rebuked the wind and the raging waters; the storm subsided, and all was calm. *"Where is your faith?"* he asked his disciples. In fear and amazement, they asked one another, "Who is this? He commands even the winds and the water, and they obey him.

Trials increase our knowledge, and they help us learn God's Word. Psalm 119:71-77: *"It was good for me to be afflicted so that I might learn your decrees. The law from your mouth is more precious to me than thousands of pieces of silver and gold. Your hands made me and formed me; give me understanding to learn your commands. May those who fear you rejoice when they see me, for I have put my hope in your word.*

I know, Lord, that your laws are righteous, and that in faithfulness you have afflicted me. May your unfailing love be my comfort, according to your promise to your servant. Let your compassion come to me that I may live, for your law is my delight." Psalm 94:11-15 *"The Lord knows all human plans; he knows that they are futile. Blessed is the one you discipline, Lord, the one you teach from your law; you grant them relief from days of trouble, till a pit is dug for the wicked. For the Lord will not reject his people; he will never forsake his inheritance. Judgment will again be founded on righteousness, and all the upright in heart will follow it."* Psalm 119:64-68 *"The earth, O Lord, is full of thy steadfast love; teach me thy statutes! Thou hast dealt well with thy servant, O Lord, according to thy word. Teach me good judgment and knowledge, for I believe in thy commandments. Before I was afflicted, I went astray; but now I keep thy word. Thou art good and doest good; teach me thy statutes."*

Trials teach us to be more thankful. 1 Thessalonians 5:16-18: *"Always be joyful. Always keep on praying. No matter what happens, always be thankful, for this is God's will for you who belong to Christ Jesus."* Ephesians 5:20: *"Giving thanks always and for everything to God the Father in the name of our Lord*

*Jesus Christ." * Colossians 4:2: *"Devote yourselves to prayer with an alert mind and a thankful heart."*

Trials take our minds off of things of the world and put them back on the Lord. Colossians 3:1-4 *"Since, then, you have been raised with Christ, set your hearts on things above, where Christ is, seated at the right hand of God. Set your minds on things above, not on earthly things. For you died, and your life is now hidden with Christ in God. When Christ, who is your life, appears, then you also will appear with him in glory."* Romans 12:1-2 *"I appeal to you therefore, brothers, by the mercies of God, to present your bodies as a living sacrifice, holy and acceptable to God, which is your spiritual worship. Do not be conformed to this world, but be transformed by the renewal of your mind, that by testing you may discern what is the will of God, what is good and acceptable and perfect."*

Stop saying, "I'm going to pray," and actually do it. Let this be a start to a new prayer life you never had. Stop thinking you can do things on your own and trust in God. Tell God, "I can't do it without you. I need you, my Lord." Come to Him with all your heart. *"God help me; I will not let you go. I will not listen to these lies."* You must stand strong and have faith God can bring you through it, even if it seems impossible.

1 Corinthians 10:13: *"No temptation has overtaken you except what is common to mankind. And God is faithful; he will not let you be tempted beyond what you can bear. But when you are tempted, he will also provide a way out so that you can endure it."*

| CHAPTER 5 |

CHOSEN FOR EXPLOITS

To embark on a journey of extraordinary achievements and accomplishments in service to the Almighty is the concept of "doing exploits for God". So, we are all chosen to perform remarkable acts that surpass the bounds of ordinary human capabilities, all while fulfilling a divine purpose. *"But the people that do know their God shall be strong and do exploits."* Daniel 11:32b.

Chosen for Exploits is a call to rise above mediocrity, embracing our potential as vessels for God's power to manifest in this world. Its essence lies in our willingness to go beyond our comfort zones and dare to dream big. Doing exploits for God requires us to tap into our inner strength of faith and courage, trusting that we can achieve extraordinary feats that transcend human limitations with His guidance. Whether we face seemingly unbelievable challenges or seize opportunities to impact lives positively, understanding this concept is crucial in living a life marked by purpose and significance.

Doing exploits for God entails going beyond ordinary actions and taking up arms against complacency. It beckons us to embrace boldness, a quality often discouraged by societal norms, and by daring greatly where others may hesitate. This boldness stems from an unwavering belief that a higher power is the Spirit of God working through us, which is the very same power that created the universe.

When we align ourselves with the Spirit of God who dwells in us, we tap into an infinite source of strength that enables us to accomplish what would otherwise be impossible. Understanding what it means to do exploits for God allows us to grasp the significance behind extraordinary acts and compels us to pursue personal growth and spiritual transformation.

It becomes an invitation to bask in the joy of our achievements and recognize the transformative journey that awaits as we dare to embrace our divine calling. Through this understanding, we embark on a path beyond mere human accomplishments, stepping into a realm where God's power works wonders and miracles become commonplace.

When we hear "exploit," our minds often conjure images of daring adventures, heroic deeds, and remarkable accomplishments. Exploits are those extraordinary feats that surpass what is considered ordinary or expected. They are the highest level of human achievement and often involve acts of bravery, skill, or intelligence that leave a lasting impact on others.

In the realm of faith and spirituality, doing exploits for God takes on a whole new dimension. It encompasses performing extraordinary acts in service to Him that go beyond what is perceived as routine or mundane.

These exploits for God can manifest in various ways, such as spreading His word with unwavering passion, selflessly helping those in need without seeking recognition, or even displaying miraculous acts of healing or deliverance. Essentially, being chosen to do exploits for God means using our God-given abilities to accomplish extraordinary things that bring glory to His name.

Doing exploits for God entails going above and beyond the call of duty to serve Him and fulfill His purposes on earth. It requires stepping out of our comfort zones and challenging ourselves to do things beyond our own perceived limitations.

Whether it be feeding the hungry, clothing the naked, advocating for justice, standing up against oppression, or leading others into a deeper relationship with Christ, all these actions fall under the umbrella of doing exploits for God. These extraordinary acts are not fueled by personal ambition or self-interest but rather by an overwhelming desire to honor and glorify God through our actions.

It is about surrendering ourselves completely to His will and allowing His power to work through us. While these exploits may seem daunting and require great faith and courage, they offer immense rewards not in earthly recognition but in the eternal impact they have on the lives of others and in deepening our relationship with God.

In a world that often settles for mediocrity, the concept of doing exploits for God challenges us to break free from the shackles of complacency and embrace a life filled with purpose, passion, and divine empowerment. It beckons us to see ourselves as vessels through which God can work wonders and bring about transformation. So, let us embark on this journey together, exploring biblical examples and uncovering the characteristics that define those who are willing to do exploits for God.

In the realm of well-known exploits for God, none is more famous than David's victory over the formidable giant, Goliath. The story takes us back to a time when the Israelites were engaged in a fierce battle against the Philistines. Goliath, a towering warrior standing over nine feet tall, challenged any Israelite soldier to face him in single combat. His taunts echoed across the battlefield, striking fear into the hearts of King Saul's army. David, however, was not like his fellow soldiers.

As a young shepherd boy chosen by God himself to become king one day, he possessed an unwavering faith that surpassed his size and strength. Armed with nothing but his sling and five smooth stones picked up from a nearby streambed, David stepped forward to confront Goliath.

It was not physical prowess alone that propelled David forward, but his unyielding belief in God's mighty power that emboldened him. Despite skepticism from King Saul and his brothers, who doubted his abilities, David remained steadfast. He declared confidently that he would prevail against this daunting adversary not by his might or strength but by God's hand.

With each step closer to Goliath, David visualized victory and how this feat would manifest as a testimony of God's faithfulness to His people. This courage, born out of trust in divine intervention, allowed him to stand resolute before an enemy seemingly insurmountable. David's triumph over Goliath went far beyond the immediate battlefield. This exploit became a symbol of hope and inspiration for generations to come.

It demonstrated that no matter how formidable the challenge is when one is chosen by God and places their trust in God, extraordinary feats can be achieved. This exploit also highlighted the power of faith in action.

David's audacity to confront and conquer a giant through sheer reliance on God inspired countless individuals to step out in faith, knowing that nothing is impossible with God on their side. The story of David and Goliath continues to resonate across time and cultures, reminding us that even the most daunting obstacles can be overcome when we possess unwavering faith in God's strength.

While not as widely recognized as David and Goliath, Elijah's exploit of calling down fire from heaven holds its own significance. The story unfolds during a dark period in Israel's history when idolatry gained a strong foothold under King Ahab's reign.

Elijah, an uncompromising prophet chosen by God, was sent to confront this spiritual decay head-on. One particular encounter took place on Mount Carmel, where Elijah challenged 450 prophets of Baal to a divine showdown. The prophets were given an opportunity to call upon their god to ignite a sacrificial offering, while Elijah did the same with the one true God. Amidst this dramatic face-off between good and evil, Elijah created an atmosphere pregnant with anticipation as both sides prepared their altars.

As time passed without any response from Baal, Elijah boldly stepped forward to address the prophets and all who were present. With unshakable certainty, he reminded the people of Israel that they were on the precipice of a divine revelation. Elijah soaked the sacrifice and the altar with water three times, emphasizing his faith and God's ability to demonstrate His power. In response to Elijah's fervent prayer, fire consumed not only the soaked sacrifice but also licked up every drop of water surrounding it.

This miraculous display left no room for doubt that God had triumphed over false idols. Through this exploit, Elijah showcased unwavering trust in God's supremacy and revealed to the nation that Yahweh alone is worthy of worship. Elijah's exploit teaches us several valuable lessons. First, it reminds us that God desires our wholehearted devotion and worship. Just as fire consumes everything in its path, so too should our passion for God be all-consuming. Second, this exploit emphasizes the importance of unwavering trust in God's power, even when circumstances seem bleak or impossible.

We learn that sometimes God chooses to work through us in extraordinary ways to reveal His might and glory. Elijah's act of calling down fire from heaven validated his prophetic ministry and inspired future generations to stand boldly against spiritual decay.

These biblical exploits demonstrate that doing exploits for God involves extraordinary acts performed with courage, faith, and unwavering trust in His power. David's victory over Goliath reminds us that no challenge is insurmountable when we place our faith in God alone.

Similarly, Elijah calling down fire from heaven reveals the transformative impact of unwavering trust and dedication to divine purpose. These stories inspire us to have audacious faith and pursue exploits for God with confidence, knowing that He empowers those who are willing to step out in obedience.

Those who do exploits for God possess a deep

faith and unwavering trust in His ability to work through them. They understand that their strength is limited, but by relying on God, they tap into a greater power. Biblical figures like Moses, Joshua, and Esther exemplify this characteristic. Despite facing seemingly impossible situations, they trusted God would guide them and provide the necessary resources.

Moses demonstrated his deep faith when leading the Israelites out of Egypt. Although initially reluctant to take on such a monumental task, he eventually trusted that God would equip him with the necessary abilities. Moses' reliance on God allowed him to perform extraordinary feats, like parting the Red Sea. Similarly, Joshua's faith in God enabled him to conquer Jericho by following unconventional instructions from the Lord.

These examples remind us that great exploits can be achieved when we completely trust Him. The implications for believers today are profound. When we cultivate a deep faith and trust in God's ability to work through us, we become vessels for His power and love to manifest in extraordinary ways. It requires stepping out of our comfort zones and surrendering control over outcomes while embracing His guidance and provision along the way. Doing exploits for God requires deep faith and purity of heart and motives. It is essential to examine the intentions behind our actions, as even remarkable accomplishments can be tainted if driven by selfish ambitions or personal gain.

Daniel is an inspiring example of someone who displayed both deep faith and purity of heart while doing exploits for God. In Babylonian captivity, Daniel steadfastly maintained his devotion to God despite facing potential harm or death due to his refusal to worship false idols. His motives were grounded in a desire to honor and glorify God rather than seeking personal recognition or safety. Daniel's integrity and purity of heart allowed God to work through him to interpret dreams, interpret supernatural handwriting on the wall, and thrive amid adversity.

For believers today, having pure intentions when doing exploits for God involves aligning ourselves with His will, seeking His glory above our own, and striving to love and serve others selflessly. It requires constantly checking our motives and surrendering any selfish desires that may hinder the purity of our actions.

As we delve into understanding what it means to do exploits for God, we discover that deep faith, trust in His power, and purity of heart are fundamental characteristics displayed by biblical figures who achieved extraordinary feats. These attributes are not confined to ancient times but hold significant implications for believers today.

When we cultivate a deep faith in God's ability to work through us and align ourselves with His will while maintaining pure motives, we become vessels through which He can perform remarkable acts. It is an invitation to step out of our comfort zones and rely on His guidance and provision while keeping our intentions grounded in love for Him.

In a world where doubt and cynicism often prevail, embracing these characteristics allows us to tap into a higher purpose and experience the joy that comes from witnessing divine intervention in our lives. So let us strive to do exploits for God with unwavering faith and pure hearts, knowing that He empowers us beyond measure.

We must engage in the journey of prayer and fasting as we seek God earnestly to do His will. As we seek His face, He has the blueprint for our lives, and we need to ask him questions. We need to find out how we can impact our families and society. We must ask Him to give us ideas, help us restructure our lives, and use us mightily to do great works of exploits for His Glory.

Throughout the Bible, we see mighty exploits done by the people of God: *"And what more shall I say? I do not have time to tell about Gideon, Barak, Samson and Jephthah, about David and Samuel and the prophets, who through faith conquered kingdoms, administered justice, and gained what was promised; who shut the mouths of lions, quenched the fury of the flames, and escaped the edge of the sword; whose weakness was turned to strength; and who became powerful in battle and routed foreign armies"* (Hebrews 11:32-34).

Daniel 11:32 teaches us that the knowledge of God combined with the strength that comes from God is the most powerful and enduring force against evil in the world. As believers, when we see what is sacred to God desecrated all around us, we cannot just sit idly by to the wonderful knowledge that our God is a strong Redeemer who fights for the vulnerable and the powerless. May we stand in awe of His wisdom and love the light and goodness that emanates from His holiness. May we love His Word and stand firm on His truth, declaring it boldly. May we listen and obey as He commands us to "Provide justice for the needy and fatherless; uphold the rights of the oppressed and the destitute. Rescue the poor and needy; save them from the power of the wicked" (Ps. 82:3-May we be like the great heroes in the faith and walk by faith and not by sight *(2 Cor. 5:7)*.

We cannot give the enemy a foothold. When the body's parts are healthy, the whole will be healthy. As we seek the Lord, He will show us, through His Spirit, how to use what's in our hands (our gifts, talents, influence, and resources) to strike a blow against this evil.

Our courage in the face of incredible odds and the rising tide of wickedness will come from knowing our God intimately. Not just knowing about Him but living in a relationship with Him and experiencing Him day-to-day. Jeremiah 9:23-24 says, *"This is what the LORD says: The wise man must not boast in his wisdom; the strong man must not boast in his strength, the wealthy man must not boast in his wealth, But the one who boasts should boast in this, that he understands and knows Me – that I am Yahweh, showing faithful love, justice, and righteousness on the earth, for I delight in these things."*

I pray that we continue in the unity of John 17 and press on in to be strong in the Lord (Eph. 6:10) and make our aim to know God and make Him known. May God position YOU this year for mighty exploits. The good news is that we don't have to figure out what to do on our own as our work is to abide and to just keep being faithful to take the next step. He leads us step by step. We just have to say, *"Yes, Lord. Whatever you have for me today, Lord, I avail myself to you."*

God is still in the business of making 'a man of valor' out of ordinary and insignificant people. The scripture says God chooses the weak things of this world to confound the things which are mighty. In preparation for battle against the Midianites, Gideon had recruited a thirty-two-thousand-man army, thinking that victory would come by the size of his army. However, God plainly told him that He didn't need that considerable number to give Israel victory in the battle. The army was eventually reduced to three hundred people because God wanted Gideon to know that the battle was the Lord's. Most believers fail woefully in life because they do not realize that no man can prevail by arms of flesh in the battles of life. As long as you feel sufficient and depend on your physical strength, wisdom, ideas, qualifications, experience, and abilities, you will find it impossible for God to supply His strength or work through you. As a mortal, you are surrounded by many limitations, but when God works through you, there is no limit to what you can achieve in life.

Another secret of Gideon's victory was that God was with him. Gideon and his three hundred men army were not trained soldiers but ordinary men who carried no weapons or knew anything about warfare. However, there was one thing they had: God was with them! It is the presence of God in a man's life that actually makes him strong and empowers him for great exploits. If God is not with you, you will be exploited by the enemies, Satan will take advantage of you at will. Unfortunately, most people still do not seek the most valuable thing in life, which is God's presence. They place emphasis on other transient things at the expense of God's presence. Acts 10:38, 'How God anointed Jesus of Nazareth with the Holy Ghost and with power: who went about doing good and healing all that were oppressed of the devil; for God was with him'. Jesus could do all that He did because God was with Him; there is no way you can do exploits in life and ministry except God is with you.

Dearly beloved, when God is fighting for you, the battles of your life become a walkover. The little efforts will yield great results. Power for great exploits is still available and accessible if you will plunge your life into the eternal source, which is God. Let God be your priority, No. 1 and only one! God is all you need! Seek Him passionately in this New Year as never before, and be committed to righteousness. Live only for His purpose, and you will see how much He can achieve through you. I see the Almighty God making a champion out of you as His chosen. You will not lose any battle anymore in life in Jesus' Mighty Name. Amen!

Heavenly Father, we thank You for the call to know You and for the strength You provide. Help us deepen our relationship with You so that we may carry out the exploits You have ordained for us as the CHOSEN children of God. Fill us with Your Holy Spirit and empower us to shine brightly in this world in the Mighty Name of Jesus, Amen.

| CHAPTER 6 |

POTENTIAL ROADBLOCKS

AVOID DISTRACTIONS

When God chooses you, you are destined to become great if you obey him and walk according to His will for your life. Do not be distracted.

Jesus didn't stay where He wasn't valued. He went to the next city, where the multitudes showed up, and many were healed. Jesus went from town to town, city to city, and village to village because He only went where He was celebrated, not where He was tolerated.

When He sent His disciples out on their own, He told them in Matthew 10:14 (NLT), *"If any household or town refuses to welcome you or listen to your message, shake its dust from your feet as you leave."*

If you're in a place where you're not being valued, very few miracles can be done. Leave there so you can go where you will be welcomed, valued, and celebrated. Never stay where you're not valued.

Always be sharp in spirit and discern the agenda of other people's direction for your life, but find the courage to follow your own heart. It will lead you to your chosen destiny. Beware! Your heart may not always follow the crowd. You must be willing to stand alone as you follow God. Another person's opinion should never override your heart. Your heart is the birthplace for your increase or your decrease. The Word of God says, *"Guard your heart above all else, for it determines the course of your life" (Proverbs 4:23, NLT).*

Some people do things so naturally that they don't even recognize that it is truly a gift or talent that is being underutilized. Knowing your gifts and creating a vision for using them is essential to becoming all you are chosen to be. Taking action is vital to your success. Don't be afraid because you're not a celebrity or people don't know you, and never allow people's perception of you and your past to stop you from God's assignment as a chosen vessel of Christ. Your job is not to open a door, as that's God's job. If you step out in faith and walk towards the door, those doors will be opened. If a door doesn't open, you may go in the wrong direction.

Don't allow the word "No" to stop you from looking for another door. If you keep going, eventually, you will get a "Yes."

People will talk about you and spread rumors with no evidence as God's chosen trying to fulfill your purpose, and even people that you trust and confide in will gang up with others to spread rumors, they have no proof of against you. You must be strong inside to resist all distractions and focus on your assignment. It doesn't come easy, but you talk less and listen more in these instances.

I think one of the main things the enemy focuses on these days is distraction. He knows that he can't always convince you to be disobedient to God, so he often sends people to say things to you to try to provoke or demand a response from you so that you are then distracted from what God has chosen you to do. Don't EVER fall for this. These are the devices of the wicked and the crafty.

Pay attention to when someone is saying something just to be provocative. People who want to give you constructive criticism or feedback will not do it in a destructive way. And remember that you don't have to explain yourself to everybody. Sometimes, people will form a whole incorrect story about you and then want you to prove to them that you're something different. Always Remember this:

If someone hears something about you that is not true, but they just automatically believe it, they want to believe it anyway. You can never control that. If someone forms an opinion about a whole situation based on a small portion of it, they aren't interested in knowing the whole story. Don't stress about this, and let it get to you.

Often, the enemy's goal is to distract you from your God-ordained purpose and focus on this loop of trying to self-justify so that you have less time and energy to focus on what God has chosen you to do.

Nehemiah 6:3 "So, I sent messengers to them, saying, *"I am doing a great work, so that I cannot come down. Why should the work cease while I leave it and go down to you?"*

Never let man take away God's divine purpose for your life by falling prey to their distractions. It may start very subtle, with you not knowing where that may lead you, and that is where the Holy Spirit will guide you in discerning their intentions. Run from those people to complete your assignment and regroup, if necessary, when done. Acts 5:29: *"But Peter and the apostles answered, We must obey God rather than men"*.

The company we keep is so important. It's hurtful to lose a friend, but the loss is really a blessing if the relationship was never authentic and genuine in the first place, and all you receive are distractions and invaluable information that isn't helping you in your walk as God's Chosen. I Corinthians 15:33 *"Do not be deceived: "Bad company ruins good morals."*

DON'T SETTLE FOR LESS

Don't listen to the voices that tell you that you must accept whatever you can get, that there's not enough, or that you can't have what God has for you. Don't listen, even if that doubtful voice is your own. All of God's promises are yes and amen. So even when we don't understand how we will do, have, or be the thing God has told us, I know Someone (God) who does understand completely, and He cannot fail.

I often must remind myself that I am a chosen daughter of The Most-High God. I won't accept any of the enemy's deceits and counterfeits that I am sometimes tempted to. But we don't want to block what God ultimately has for us because we lack the patience or faith to believe that He will do what He said. Ephesians 3:20-21: *"Now unto him that is able to do exceedingly abundantly above all that we ask or think, according to the power that worketh in us, unto him be glory in the church by Christ Jesus throughout all ages, world without end."* Amen.

Sometimes, you're doing the right thing, and the enemy wishes you wouldn't so that the enemy doesn't have to face the guilt they have concerning the narrative they have created about you. Even when those around you choose to let fear lead them, you can make a different choice as God's chosen. II Timothy 1:7: *"For God has not given us a spirit of fear, but of power and of love and of a sound mind."*

Observe what people do, but listen to what they say, too. We ought to be kind to each other. But kindness does not require us to be enablers or doormats. Love is compassion and understanding but also includes appropriate boundaries and accountability. We don't have to let ourselves be destroyed to build up another person. Luke 6:45: *"A good man out of the good treasure of his heart brings forth good; and an evil man out of the evil treasure of his heart brings forth evil. For out of the abundance of the heart, his mouth speaks."*

Often, I have heard forgiveness conflated with restoration to the same level of access. By the grace of God, we can forgive others of even horrific things.

However, forgiveness does not necessarily come with the restoration of the relationship. Sometimes, it's unsafe to do so.

I am a follower of Christ. But let's not get it confused. That doesn't mean that I must bow to abuse or perpetual mistreatment. I can end the relationship or set boundaries in grace and still hold no ill will for the other person. If I trusted someone to babysit for me while I'm out of town and I return to a house with the caretaker chatting on the phone and a baby who has not been fed for hours, crying and a diaper so full, then I can't trust that person again to take care of my precious baby. I can forgive them, but they can't come back to my house to care for my child. Where there is no evidence of true repentance, we sometimes must cut ties to prevent further harm.

It's wonderful when restoration is possible. But sometimes it's not, and that's okay too. Romans 12:18: *"If it is possible, as much as depends on you, live peaceably with all men."*

The enemy recruited someone who had access to me to spread a lot of wild rumors about me. I cannot begin to describe it here. All hell broke loose, but the Lord gave me strength and wisdom to handle the situation. It wasn't an easy situation, but beware, as when God chooses you, the enemy will plant people very close to you to sow seeds of turbulence and confusion around you, but with closeness to the Holy Spirit and discernment, the Lord will guide you. They tried everything, but it sure didn't work. I am still standing. Genesis 50:20: *"But as for you, ye thought evil against me; but God meant it unto good, to bring to pass, as it is this day, to save much people alive."*

LEARN TO HEAR GOD'S VOICE

When God gives us instructions, He does not ask us to do it when we feel it should be done or when circumstances align comfortably. He is asking us to trust Him. Part of walking in faith is being willing to walk out on the water when we are called, even when that seems to be the least sensible option. To follow God's voice, though, we need to recognize it.

The decisions we make as God's chosen are so critical to the quality of our lives. As believers, we want the best that God has for us. That means we must be diligent about learning to hear God's voice clearly and distinguish it from others. When I hear a prompting, I always try to ask, is this God, the devil, or me speaking? Distinguishing between the voices that speak to us daily is vital to remain on God's path. Our Father is constantly trying to guide and direct our lives and to act on and obey His voice; we need to discern it from the other voices. John 10:27-28 *"My sheep hear my voice, and I know them, and they follow me. I give them eternal life, and they will never perish, and no one will snatch them out of my hand"*.

God will never say anything that is contrary to His Word. When Eve was tempted, the serpent did one thing, which was to contradict what God had said. Satan distorts God's Word, and we must compare everything we hear with what the commands of God are. Our best defense is to know the Bible and what God says about us, the world, and the devil. If you want to sharpen your sensitivity to the voice of the Lord, spend time and cultivate daily study time and reading of His Word.

We all have emotions that can, sometimes, get out of control and start to distract us. We can see pictures in our minds when we get overwhelmed, and this may not be from God. We need to settle our human emotions and enter the presence of God by worshiping and meditating on His Word. After you usher yourself into the presence of God, you need to ask what the inner witness or voice from your spirit is saying. The Holy Spirit speaks into our spirits, and the voice of God will provide illumination and direction in that particular area of our lives. This is why quieting and yielding yourself to God is so essential. God will light the lamp, and the lamp will provide light, and the light will provide illumination.

Whenever there is an unsettling feeling about what an internal voice is saying, then it is not the voice of God. God will not give you doubt or tension because when He is leading you, He will use His peace to confirm His perfect will. When your circumstances line up in a supernatural way, then that is a sign that the Lord is speaking to you and moving on your behalf. It is also important to note that if you sense spiritual warfare in a matter that you believe God spoke to you about, then that is a good indication you are walking in God's will. Your spirit will bear witness with God's spirit.

SETTING BOUNDARIES
Setting boundaries is essential for personal well-being and fulfilling one's divine calling as a chosen child of God. There is a desire for approval and the need for validation or acceptance from others can lead to overextending oneself and neglecting personal limits. Proverbs 25:17 "Seldom set foot in your neighbor's house—too much of you, and they will hate you." This

verse emphasizes the importance of knowing when to step back and maintain personal space.

Some may feel guilty about saying no or disappointing others, believing that they should always be available or accommodating.

Galatians 6:5: *"For each will have to bear his own load."* This reminds us that while we can support others, we are ultimately responsible for our own responsibilities.

The desire to be perfect or to meet every expectation can inhibit the ability to set necessary limits, as individuals may believe they must do it all. Matthew 5:37: "Let what you say be simply 'Yes' or 'No' as anything more than this comes from evil. Clear communication is key to setting boundaries. Be firm and direct in your responses.

When overwhelmed by responsibilities or emotions, individuals may struggle to identify and communicate their boundaries effectively. 1 Corinthians 15:33: "Do not be misled: 'Bad company corrupts good character.' Surrounding yourself with the right people is crucial. Establish boundaries with those who may negatively influence you. Accept people for who they are, but place them where they belong in your life.

Negative past experiences with boundary-setting,

such as being punished or ridiculed for asserting oneself, can create hesitancy in future situations. Romans 12:18: *"If possible, so far as it depends on you, live peaceably with all."* While it's important to seek peace, it's also vital to recognize when to create distance for your own peace.

Individuals with low self-worth may feel that their needs are less important than those of others, making it difficult to prioritize their own boundaries. Philippians 4:13: "I can do all things through him who strengthens me." Trust in God's strength as you set and maintain boundaries to fulfill your calling.

The belief that setting boundaries may lead to loneliness or the loss of relationships can deter individuals from asserting their limits. Psalm 119:35: "Lead me in the path of your commandments, for I delight in it." Setting boundaries can help you stay aligned with God's purpose for your life as the chosen of Christ. You must build a foundation for establishing and maintaining boundaries that support your calling and personal growth.

There's not necessarily a one-size-fits-all way to set boundaries when dealing with a person operating in the spirit of control because it presents in different types of relationships, and the circumstances are different.

For example, you handle your supervisor at work differently than you interact with your spouse. You communicate with a peer or a friend differently than your parents. And you move differently when you're in a situation that is uncomfortable versus an abusive situation.

DOUBT AND FEAR

Doubt and fear are weapons that can kill a dream and stop a beautiful vision right in its tracks. When God chooses you and gives you a vision, we must agree with what He has said. Be careful who you share the vision with, as you need people who will stand in agreement and not give you different new ideas about how everything could go wrong. I trust the Lord, but I am imperfect. So, if I do not steward God's vision well and let contrary words seep in, I could end up doubting God and His plan.

I don't hold anything against those who are naysayers, the negative, and the pessimistic. I pray that the joy of the Lord enters their hearts and that they see that God has a purpose and plan for their lives, too. In many cases, I can still have some level of relationship with them. But the vision God gives me, I must keep that part away from them. For faith's sake,

I set boundaries so that the vision can come to pass. James 1:6-8 *"But let him ask in faith, with no doubting, for he who doubts is like a wave of the sea driven and tossed by the wind. For let not that man suppose that he will receive anything from the Lord; he is a double-minded man, unstable in all his ways."*

You need to make the decision to live again after disappointment, failures, or things not going as planned. God is in the business of second, third, fourth, and seventieth chances to start over and get it right. Don't let the enemy keep you in a place of stagnation or fear. Many people are merely existing. Existing, by definition, means to be present at the time. God wants you to live! To live means to be in motion. You need to realize it doesn't matter what is going on in the present. You have a future that God predetermined before you were conceived. Your future is far greater than your present circumstances.

Job was a man who suffered more than most of us. He lost his business, wealth, children, and health. His friends accused him of bringing it all upon himself. His wife told him to curse God for everything and just give up. Job made a choice to remain steadfast in his faith and belief in the God he served. God rewarded his faith and perseverance in the face of tribulation.

Deciding to live again sometimes means hitting the restart button. We may feel like we are already behind in life and that starting over will put us even further behind, but that couldn't be further from the truth. Instead of trying to fix something broken, starting over can propel us toward becoming the best version of ourselves.

Celebrate your life, not your possessions. When you're starting over with nothing, you have no reputation. Jesus said He wasn't trying to make Himself famous. He came to do what the Father had purposed for His life. He put others ahead of Him, which you should also do. Just because you are chosen for a great job doesn't mean you are not going to make mistakes or find yourself in desperate situations. It does mean that God's hand is on your life and that grace is following you to protect you.

CHAPTER 7

SCRIPTURES ON CHOSEN

1 Peter 2:9 ESV

But you are a chosen race, a royal priesthood, a holy nation, a people for his own possession, that you may proclaim the excellencies of him who called you out of darkness into his marvelous light.

John 15:16 ESV

You did not choose me, but I chose you and appointed you that you should go and bear fruit and that your fruit should abide, so that whatever you ask the Father in my name, he may give it to you.

Jeremiah 1:5 ESV

Before I formed you in the womb I knew you, and before you were born, I consecrated you; I appointed you a prophet to the nations.

Ephesians 1:3-4 ESV

Blessed be the God and Father of our Lord Jesus Christ, who has blessed us in Christ with every spiritual blessing in the heavenly places, even as he chose us in him before the foundation of the world, that we should be holy and blameless before him in love.

Deuteronomy 14:2 ESV

For you are a people holy to the LORD your God, and the LORD has chosen you to be a people for his treasured possession, out of all the peoples who are on the face of the earth.

John 3:16 ESV

For God so loved the world, that he gave his only Son, that whoever believes in him should not perish but have eternal life.

Isaiah 43:10 ESV

You are my witnesses, declares the LORD, and my servant whom I have chosen, that you may know and believe me and understand that I am he. Before me no god was formed, nor shall there be any after me.

Matthew 22:14 ESV
For many are called, but few are chosen.

2 Thessalonians 2:14 ESV
To this he called you through our gospel, so that you may obtain the glory of our Lord Jesus Christ.

1 Thessalonians 1:4 ESV
For we know, brothers loved by God, that he has chosen you,

1 John 2:27 ESV
But the anointing that you received from him abides in you, and you have no need that anyone should teach you. But as his anointing teaches you about everything, and is true, and is no lie—just as it has taught you, abide in him.

Psalm 82:6 ESV
I said, "You are gods, sons of the Most-High, all of you.

John 13:19 ESV
I am telling you this now, before it takes place, that when it does take place, you may believe that I am He.

John 16:13 ESV

When the Spirit of truth comes, he will guide you into all the truth, for he will not speak on his own authority, but whatever he hears he will speak, and he will declare to you the things that are to come.

John 6:44 ESV

No one can come to me unless the Father who sent me draws him. And I will raise him up on the last day.

Jeremiah 1:4-5 ESV

Now the word of the LORD came to me, saying, "Before I formed you in the womb I knew you, and before you were born, I consecrated you; I appointed you a prophet to the nations."

1 John 1:9 ESV

If we confess our sins, he is faithful and just to forgive us our sins and to cleanse us from all unrighteousness.

John 14:6 ESV

Jesus said to him, "I am the way, and the truth, and the life. No one comes to the Father except through me.

Jeremiah 29:11 ESV

For I know the plans I have for you, declares the LORD,

plans for welfare and not for evil, to give you a future and a hope.

Revelation 13:8 ESV

And all who dwell on earth will worship it, everyone whose name has not been written before the foundation of the world in the book of life of the Lamb who was slain.

Romans 8:28 ESV

And we know that for those who love God all things work together for good, for those who are called according to his purpose.

Isaiah 43:1-3 ESV

But now thus says the LORD, he who created you, O Jacob, he who formed you, O Israel: "Fear not, for I have redeemed you; I have called you by name, you are mine. When you pass through the waters, I will be with you; and through the rivers, they shall not overwhelm you; when you walk through fire you shall not be burned, and the flame shall not consume you. For I am the LORD your God, the Holy One of Israel, your Savior. I give Egypt as your ransom, Cush and Seba in exchange for you.

Deuteronomy 7:6 ESV

For you are a people holy to the LORD your God. The LORD your God has chosen you to be a people for his treasured possession, out of all the peoples who are on the face of the earth.

Matthew 6:24 ESV

No one can serve two masters, for either he will hate the one and love the other, or he will be devoted to the one and despise the other. You cannot serve God and money.

John 6:37 ESV

All that the Father gives me will come to me, and whoever comes to me I will never cast out.

Exodus 19:5 ESV

Now therefore, if you will indeed obey my voice and keep my covenant, you shall be my treasured possession among all peoples, for all the earth is mine.

2 Thessalonians 2:13 ESV

But we ought always to give thanks to God for you, brothers beloved by the Lord, because God chose you as the first fruits to be saved, through sanctification by the Spirit and belief in the truth.

Ephesians 2:8-9 ESV

For by grace, you have been saved through faith. And this is not your own doing; it is the gift of God, not a result of works, so that no one may boast.

Romans 6:23 ESV

For the wages of sin is death, but the free gift of God is eternal life in Christ Jesus our Lord.

Galatians 1:15-16 ESV

But when he who had set me apart before I was born, and who called me by his grace, was pleased to reveal his Son to me, in order that I might preach him among the Gentiles, I did not immediately consult with anyone.

Exodus 19:6 ESV

And you shall be to me a kingdom of priests and a holy nation. These are the words that you shall speak to the people of Israel."

Ephesians 2:10 ESV

For we are his workmanship, created in Christ Jesus

for good works, which God prepared beforehand, that we should walk in them.

John 6:40-41 ESV

For this is the will of my Father, that everyone who looks on the Son and believes in him should have eternal life, and I will raise him up on the last day." So, the Jews grumbled about him, because he said, "I am the bread that came down from heaven."

Psalm 45:7 ESV

You have loved righteousness and hated wickedness. Therefore God, your God, has anointed you with the oil of gladness beyond your companions.

Jeremiah 5:22 ESV

Do you not fear me? declares the LORD. Do you not tremble before me? I placed the sand as the boundary for the sea, a perpetual barrier that it cannot pass; though the waves toss, they cannot prevail; though they roar, they cannot pass over it.

1 Peter 1:2 ESV

According to the foreknowledge of God the Father, in

the sanctification of the Spirit, for obedience to Jesus Christ and for sprinkling with his blood: May grace and peace be multiplied to you.

Ephesians 1:4-5
Even as he chose us in him before the foundation of the world, that we should be holy and blameless before him. In love he predestined us for adoption as sons through Jesus Christ, according to the purpose of his will.

Genesis 12:1-3 ESV
Now the LORD said to Abram, "Go from your country and your kindred and your father's house to the land that I will show you. And I will make you a great nation, and I will bless you and make your name great, so that you will be a blessing. I will bless those who bless you, and him who dishonors you I will curse, and in you all the families of the earth shall be blessed."

Colossians 3:12 ESV
Put on then, as God's chosen ones, holy and beloved, compassionate hearts, kindness, humility, meekness, and patience.

Romans 11:5 ESV

So too at the present time there is a remnant, chosen by grace.

Galatians 1:15 ESV

But when he who had set me apart before I was born, and who called me by his grace.

Luke 1:37 ESV

For nothing will be impossible with God.

Revelation 17:14 ESV

They will make war on the Lamb, and the Lamb will conquer them, for he is Lord of lords and King of kings, and those with him are called and chosen and faithful.

Isaiah 6:8 ESV

And I heard the voice of the Lord saying, "Whom shall I send, and who will go for us?" Then I said, "Here am I! Send me."

Acts 13:48 ESV

And when the Gentiles heard this, they began rejoicing and glorifying the word of the Lord, and as many as were appointed to eternal life believed.

Titus 2:14 ESV

Who gave himself for us to redeem us from all lawlessness and to purify for himself a people for his own possession who are zealous for good works.

Luke 2:21 ESV

And at the end of eight days, when he was circumcised, he was called Jesus, the name given by the angel before he was conceived in the womb.

Isaiah 9:6 ESV

For to us a child is born, to us a son is given; and the government shall be upon his shoulder, and his name shall be called Wonderful Counselor, Mighty God, Everlasting Father, Prince of Peace.

Romans 8:28-30 ESV

And we know that for those who love God all things work together for good, for those who are called according to his purpose. For those whom he foreknew he also predestined to be conformed to the image of his Son, in order that he might be the firstborn among many brothers. And those whom he predestined he also called, and those whom he called he also justified, and those whom he justified he also glorified.

Psalm 135:4 ESV
For the LORD has chosen Jacob for himself, Israel as his own possession.

Ephesians 1:11 ESV
In him we have obtained an inheritance, having been predestined according to the purpose of him who works all things according to the counsel of his will,

Acts 3:15 ESV
And you killed the Author of life, whom God raised from the dead. To this we are witnesses.

Romans 8:30 ESV
And those whom he predestined he also called, and those whom he called he also justified, and those whom he justified he also glorified.

Luke 18:7 ESV
And will not God give justice to his elect, who cry to him day and night? Will he delay long over them?

Revelation 3:20 ESV

Behold, I stand at the door and knock. If anyone hears my voice and opens the door, I will come into him and eat with him, and he with me.

2 Timothy 2:10 ESV

Therefore, I endure everything for the sake of the elect, that they also may obtain the salvation that is in Christ Jesus with eternal glory.

Matthew 26:28 ESV

For this is my blood of the covenant, which is poured out for many for the forgiveness of sins.

Ephesians 2:19 ESV

So, then you are no longer strangers and aliens, but you are fellow citizens with the saints and members of the household of God.

Galatians 2:20 ESV

I have been crucified with Christ. It is no longer I who live, but Christ who lives in me. And the life I now live in the flesh I live by faith in the Son of God, who loved me and gave himself for me.

John 10:30 ESV
I and the Father are one.

Deuteronomy 7:6-8 ESV
For you are a people holy to the LORD your God. The LORD your God has chosen you to be a people for his treasured possession, out of all the peoples who are on the face of the earth. It was not because you were more in number than any other people that the LORD set his love on you and chose you, for you were the fewest of all peoples, but it is because the LORD loves you and is keeping the oath that he swore to your fathers, that the LORD has brought you out with a mighty hand and redeemed you from the house of slavery, from the hand of Pharaoh king of Egypt.

Romans 8:6 ESV
For to set the mind on the flesh is death, but to set the mind on the Spirit is life and peace.

John 6:65 ESV
And he said, "This is why I told you that no one can come to me unless it is granted him by the Father."

Matthew 7:13-14 ESV

"Enter by the narrow gate. For the gate is wide and the way is easy that leads to destruction, and those who enter by it are many. For the gate is narrow and the way is hard that leads to life, and those who find it are few.

Deuteronomy 30:1-8 ESV

"And when all these things come upon you, the blessing and the curse, which I have set before you, and you call them to mind among all the nations where the LORD your God has driven you, and return to the LORD your God, you and your children, and obey his voice in all that I command you today, with all your heart and with all your soul, then the LORD your God will restore your fortunes and have compassion on you, and he will gather you again from all the peoples where the LORD your God has scattered you. If your outcasts are in the uttermost parts of heaven, from there the LORD your God will gather you, and from there he will take you. And the LORD your God will bring you into the land that your fathers possessed, that you may possess it. And he will make you more prosperous and numerous than your fathers.

Galatians 3:29 ESV

And if you are Christ's, then you are Abraham's offspring, heirs according to promise.

Psalm 33:12 ESV

Blessed is the nation whose God is the LORD, the people whom he has chosen as his heritage!

Nehemiah 4:14 ESV

And I looked and arose and said to the nobles and to the officials and to the rest of the people, "Do not be afraid of them. Remember the Lord, who is great and awesome, and fight for your brothers, your sons, your daughters, your wives, and your homes."

John 6:70 ESV

Jesus answered them, "Did I not choose you, the Twelve? And yet one of you is a devil."

John 5:30 ESV

"I can do nothing on my own. As I hear, I judge, and my judgment is just because I seek not my own will but the will of him who sent me.

1 Peter 1:1 ESV

Peter, an apostle of Jesus Christ, To those who are elect exiles of the dispersion in Pontus, Galatia, Cappadocia, Asia, and Bithynia,

Colossians 3:12-17 ESV

Put on then, as God's chosen ones, holy and beloved, compassionate hearts, kindness, humility, meekness, and patience, bearing with one another and, if one has a complaint against another, forgiving each other; as the Lord has forgiven you, so you also must forgive. And above all these put-on love, which binds everything together in perfect harmony. And let the peace of Christ rule in your hearts, to which indeed you were called in one body. And be thankful. Let the word of Christ dwell in you richly, teaching and admonishing one another in all wisdom, singing psalms and hymns and spiritual songs, with thankfulness in your hearts to God.

Ephesians 2:9 ESV

Not a result of works, so that no one may boast.

Matthew 7:21-23 ESV

"Not everyone who says to me, 'Lord, Lord,' will enter the kingdom of heaven, but the one who does the will

of my Father who is in heaven. On that day many will say to me, 'Lord, Lord, did we not prophesy in your name, and cast out demons in your name, and do many mighty works in your name?' And then will I declare to them, 'I never knew you; depart from me, you workers of lawlessness.'

2 Chronicles 7:14 ESV
If my people who are called by my name humble themselves and pray and seek my face and turn from their wicked ways, then I will hear from heaven and will forgive their sin and heal their land.

Hebrews 11:10 ESV
For he was looking forward to the city that has foundations, whose designer and builder is God.

Philippians 4:13 ESV
I can do all things through him who strengthens me.

Romans 12:2 ESV
Do not be conformed to this world, but be transformed by the renewal of your mind, that by testing you may discern what is the will of God, what is good and acceptable and perfect.

Matthew 7:12 ESV

"So, whatever you wish that others would do to you, do also to them, for this is the Law and the Prophets.

Isaiah 43:1 ESV

But now thus says the LORD, he who created you, O Jacob, he who formed you, O Israel: "Fear not, for I have redeemed you; I have called you by name, you are mine.

Romans 9:11 ESV

Though they were not yet born and had done nothing either good or bad—in order that God's purpose of election might continue, not because of works but because of him who calls—

Romans 8:29 ESV

For those whom he foreknew he also predestined to be conformed to the image of his Son, in order that he might be the firstborn among many brothers.

Isaiah 41:10 ESV

Fear not, for I am with you; be not dismayed, for I am your God; I will strengthen you, I will help you, I will uphold you with my righteous right hand.

Isaiah 41:8 ESV
But you, Israel, my servant, Jacob, whom I have chosen, the offspring of Abraham, my friend.

2 Thessalonians 2:13-15 ESV
But we ought always to give thanks to God for you, brothers beloved by the Lord, because God chose you as the first fruits to be saved, through sanctification by the Spirit and belief in the truth. To this he called you through our gospel, so that you may obtain the glory of our Lord Jesus Christ. So then, brothers, stand firm and hold to the traditions that you were taught by us, either by our spoken word or by our letter.

1 Timothy 2:4 ESV
Who desires all people to be saved and to come to the knowledge of the truth.

Galatians 3:7 ESV
Know then that it is those of faith who are the sons of Abraham.

John 3:16-17 ESV

"For God so loved the world, that he gave his only Son, that whoever believes in him should not perish but have eternal life. For God did not send his Son into the world to condemn the world, but in order that the world might be saved through him.

1 Chronicles 16:11 ESV

Seek the LORD and his strength; seek his presence continually!

2 Corinthians 5:17 ESV

Therefore, if anyone is in Christ, he is a new creation. The old has passed away; behold, the new has come.

John 1:1 ESV

In the beginning was the Word, and the Word was with God, and the Word was God.

Matthew 21:43 ESV

Therefore, I tell you, the kingdom of God will be taken away from you and given to a people producing its fruits.

2 Peter 2:5 ESV

If he did not spare the ancient world, but preserved Noah, a herald of righteousness, with seven others, when he brought a flood upon the world of the ungodly.

Hebrews 11:1 ESV

Now faith is the assurance of things hoped for, the conviction of things not seen.

Proverbs 27:17 ESV

Iron sharpens iron, and one man sharpens another.

1 Peter 2:5 ESV

You yourselves like living stones are being built up as a spiritual house, to be a holy priesthood, to offer spiritual sacrifices acceptable to God through Jesus Christ.

Leviticus 19:2 ESV

"Speak to all the congregation of the people of Israel and say to them, You shall be holy, for I the LORD your God am holy.

CHAPTER 8

PRAYERS FOR THE CHOSEN

1. Oh Lord, forgive me in any way that I have let you down in the Mighty Name of Jesus.

2. Oh Lord, send your fire into the foundation of my life and let every enemy of my calling disappear in the Mighty Name of Jesus.

3. Oh Lord, let the spirit of rebellion in me disappear so I can fulfill your purpose in the Mighty Name of Jesus.

4. Oh Lord, purge me with your fire and change me to your best today in the Mighty Name of Jesus.

5. Oh Lord, send your fire into the root of my life; let every enemy of my calling scatter in the name of

Jesus.

6. Oh Lord, let your fire of deliverance fall upon me in the Name of Jesus.

7. Oh Lord, let your fire of revival fall upon me in the Name of Jesus.

8. Oh Lord, let your fire touch my spirit, soul, and body in the Name of Jesus.

9. Oh Lord, reveal to me Your purpose for my calling in the Name of Jesus.

10. Oh Lord, as you have chosen me, direct my path in the Name of Jesus.

11. Oh Lord, grant me clarity in understanding my purpose and calling. Help me to see the path you have set before me in the Name of Jesus.

12. Oh God, give me the strength and courage to follow your calling, even when the path is challenging. Help me to trust in your plan in the Name of Jesus.

13. Heavenly Father, impart your wisdom upon me as I navigate my journey. Let me make decisions that align with your will in the Name of Jesus.

14. Oh Lord, protect me from distractions and negative influences that may hinder my calling. Surround me with your angels and keep me safe in the Name of Jesus.

15. Oh Lord, help me to trust in you completely. Strengthen my faith as I pursue the purpose you have for me in the Name of Jesus.

16. Oh Lord, bring the right people into my life who will support and encourage me in my journey. Let our paths cross for your glory in the Name of Jesus.

17. Oh Lord, grant me perseverance to endure through trials and challenges. Remind me that my struggles are part of your greater plan in the Name of Jesus.

18. Oh Lord, help me to remain humble and recognize that my calling is not for my glory but for your purpose and the benefit of others in the Name of Jesus.

19. Oh Lord, nurture my spirit and help me grow in my relationship with you. Let me seek you daily and be filled with your love and guidance in the Name of Jesus.

20. Oh Lord, I claim the promises you have made. Help me to walk in faith and see your promises fulfilled in my life in the Name of Jesus.

21. Oh Lord, reveal to me the specific calling you have placed on my life. Help me to understand the purpose you have designed for me in the Name of Jesus.

22. Oh Lord, grant me the strength and endurance to pursue my calling, especially during challenging times. Help me to remain steadfast in my journey in the Name of Jesus.

23. Oh Lord, guide my steps, Lord. Illuminate the path I should take and provide me with clarity in every decision I make related to my calling in the Name of Jesus.

24. Oh Lord, provide me with the necessary financial, emotional, and spiritual resources to fulfill my divine calling. Let nothing hinder my purpose in the Name of Jesus.

25. Oh Lord, instill in me the confidence and boldness to step out in faith and pursue my calling without fear. Help me to trust in your power working through me in the Name of Jesus.

26. Oh Lord, help me to develop the skills and talents I need to fulfill my calling. Lead me to opportunities for growth and learning in the Name of Jesus.

27. Oh Lord, bring mentors, friends, and supporters into my life who will encourage and uplift me as I walk in my calling. Surround me with a community of faith, in Jesus' name.

28. Oh Lord, help me to overcome any doubts or insecurities that may hinder my progress. Remind me that I am chosen and equipped for this purpose in the Name of Jesus.

29. Oh Lord, may my desires align with your will.

Help me to seek your kingdom first and trust that all other things will fall into place in the Name of Jesus.

30. Oh Lord, grant me the grace to be faithful in my calling, even when the journey becomes difficult. May I always seek to glorify you in all I do in the Name of Jesus.

| CHAPTER 9 |

DECLARATIONS & DECREES: YOU ARE CHOSEN OF GOD!

- I decree, and I declare I am Chosen as Christ's faithful one *(Ephesians 1:1)*.

- I decree, and I declare I am God's Chosen child *(John 1:12)*.

- I decree, and I declare I have been Chosen as justified *(Romans 5:1)*.

- I decree, and I declare I am Christ's Chosen friend *(John 15:15)*.

- I decree, and I declare I am Chosen and belong to God *(1 Corinthians 6:20)*.

- I decree, and I declare I am a Chosen member of Christ's Body *(1 Corinthians 12:27).*

- I decree, and I declare I am assured all things work together for good for God's Chosen *(Romans 8:28).*

- I decree, and I declare I have been established, anointed, and sealed by God as God's Chosen *(2 Corinthians 1:21-22).*

- I decree, and I declare I am confident as God's Chosen that God will perfect the work He has begun in me *(Philippians 1:6).*

- I decree, and I declare I am God's Chosen and a citizen of Heaven *(Philippians 3:20).*

- I decree, and I declare I am God's Chosen hidden with Christ in God *(Colossians 3:3).*

- I decree and declare as God's Chosen, I have not been given a spirit of fear, but of power, love, and self-discipline *(2 Timothy 1:7).*

- I decree, and I declare I am born of God, and the evil one cannot touch God's Chosen *(1 John 5:18)*.

- I decree, and I declare I am blessed in the heavenly realms with every spiritual blessing as God's Chosen *(Ephesians 1:3)*.

- I decree, and I declare I am God's Chosen before the creation of the world *(Ephesians 1:4, 11)*.

- I decree, and I declare I am God's Chosen, and I am holy and blameless *(Ephesians 1:4)*.

- I decree, and I declare I am adopted as God's Chosen and His child *(Ephesians 1:5)*.

- I decree, and I declare I am God's Chosen, and I have been given God's glorious grace lavishly and without restriction *(Ephesians 1:5,8)*.

- I decree, and I declare I am God's Chosen in Him *(Ephesians 1:7; 1 Corinthians 1:30)*.

- I decree, and I declare I have redemption as God's Chosen *(Ephesians 1:8)*.

- I decree, and I declare I am God's Chosen and forgiven *(Ephesians 1:8; Colossians 1:14)*.

- I decree, and I declare I have a purpose as God's Chosen *(Ephesians 1:9 & 3:11)*.

- I decree, and I declare I have hope as God's Chosen *(Ephesians 1:12)*.

- I decree, and I declare I am included as God's Chosen *(Ephesians 1:13)*.

- I decree, and I declare I am sealed with the promised Holy Spirit as God's Chosen *(Ephesians 1:13)*.

- I decree, and I declare I am God's Chosen and a saint *(Ephesians 1:18)*.

- I decree, and I declare I am God's Chosen and the salt and light of the earth *(Matthew 5:13-14)*.

- I decree, and I declare I have been Chosen, and God desires me to bear fruit *(John 15:1,5)*.

- I decree and declare I am God's Chosen and a personal witness of Jesus Christ *(Acts 1:8)*.

- I decree, and I declare I am God's Chosen and His co-worker *(2 Corinthians 6:1)*.

- I decree, and I declare I am God's Chosen and a minister of reconciliation *(2 Corinthians 5:17-20)*.

- I decree and declare I am God's Chosen and alive with Christ *(Ephesians 2:5)*.

- I decree and declare I am raised with Christ as God's Chosen *(Ephesians 2:6; Colossians 2:12)*.

- I decree, and I declare I am God's Chosen who is seated with Christ in the heavenly realms *(Ephesians 2:6)*.

- I decree, and I declare I have been shown the incomparable riches of God's grace as God's Chosen *(Ephesians 2:7)*.

- I decree, and I declare God has Chosen me and expressed His kindness to me *(Ephesians 2:7)*.

- I decree, and I declare I am God's Chosen and His workmanship *(Ephesians 2:10)*.

- I decree, and I declare I have been brought near to God through Christ's blood as God's Chosen *(Ephesians 2:13)*.

- I decree, and I declare I have peace as God's Chosen *(Ephesians 2:14)*.

- I decree, and I declare I am God's Chosen, and I have access to the Father *(Ephesians 2:18)*.

- I decree, and I declare I am a Chosen member of God's household *(Ephesians 2:19)*.

- I decree, and I declare I am God's Chosen and secured child *(Ephesians 2:20)*.

- I decree, and I declare I am God's Chosen and a holy temple *(Ephesians 2:21; 1 Corinthians 6:19)*.

- I decree, and I declare I am God's Chosen and a dwelling for the Holy Spirit *(Ephesians 2:22)*.

- I decree, and I declare I am God's Chosen, and I share in the promise of Christ Jesus *(Ephesians 3:6).*

- I decree, and I declare God's power works through me as God's Chosen *(Ephesians 3:7).*

- I decree, and I declare I can approach God with freedom and confidence as God's Chosen *(Ephesians 3:12).*

- I decree, and I declare I know there is a purpose for my sufferings as God's Chosen *(Ephesians 3:13).*

- I decree, and I declare I am God's Chosen, and I can grasp how wide, long, high, and deep Christ's love is *(Ephesians 3:18).*

- I decree, and I declare I am God's Chosen and completed by God *(Ephesians 3:19).*

- I decree, and I declare I am God's Chosen, and I can bring glory to God *(Ephesians 3:21).*

- I decree, and I declare I am God's Chosen, and I

have been called *(Ephesians 4:1; 2 Timothy 1:9).*

- I decree, and I declare I am God's Chosen, and I can be humble, gentle, patient, and lovingly tolerant of others *(Ephesians 4:2).*

- I decree, and I declare I am God's Chosen, and I can mature spiritually *(Ephesians 4:15).*

- I decree, and I declare I am God's Chosen, and I can be certain of God's truths and the lifestyle that He has called me to. *(Ephesians 4:17).*

- I decree and declare I am God's Chosen, and I can have a new attitude and lifestyle *(Ephesians 4:21-32).*

- I decree, and I declare I am God's Chosen, and I can be kind and compassionate to others *(Ephesians 4:32).*

- I decree, and I declare I am God's Chosen, and I can forgive others *(Ephesians 4:32).*

- I decree, and I declare I am God's Chosen and a light

to others and can exhibit goodness, righteousness, and truth *(Ephesians 5:8-9)*.

- I decree, and I declare I am God's Chosen, and I can understand what God's will is *(Ephesians 5:17)*.

- I decree, and I declare I am God's Chosen, and I can give thanks for everything *(Ephesians 5:20)*.

- I decree, and I declare I am God's Chosen, and I don't have to always have my own agenda *(Ephesians 5:21)*.

- I decree, and I declare I am God's Chosen, and I can honor God through marriage *(Ephesians 5:22-33)*.

- I decree, and I declare I am God's Chosen, and I can parent my children with composure *(Ephesians 6:4)*.

- I decree, and I declare I am God's Chosen, and I can be strong *(Ephesians 6:10)*.

- I decree, and I declare I am God's Chosen, and I have God's power *(Ephesians 6:10)*.

- I decree, and I declare I am God's Chosen, and I can stand firm in the day of evil *(Ephesians 6:13)*.

- I decree, and I declare I am God's Chosen, and I am dead to sin *(Romans 1:12)*.

- I decree, and I declare I am God's Chosen, and I am not alone *(Hebrews 13:5)*.

- I decree, and I declare I am God's Chosen, and I am growing *(Colossians 2:7)*.

- I decree, and I declare I am God's Chosen, and I am His disciple *(John 13:15)*.

- I decree, and I declare I am God's Chosen, and I am prayed for by Jesus Christ *(John 17:20-23)*.

- I decree, and I declare I am God's Chosen, and I am united with other believers *(John 17:20-23)*.

- I decree, and I declare I am God's Chosen, and I am not in want *(Philippians 4:19)*.

- I decree, and I declare I am God's Chosen, and I

possess the mind of Christ *(I Corinthians 2:16)*.

- I decree, and I declare I am God's Chosen, and I am promised eternal life *(John 6:47)*.

- I decree, and I declare I am God's Chosen, and I am promised a full life *(John 10:10)*.

- I decree, and I declare I am God's Chosen, and I live a victorious life *(I John 5:4)*.

- I decree, and I declare I am God's Chosen, and my heart and mind are protected with God's peace *(Philippians 4:7)*.

- I decree, and I declare I am God's Chosen, and I am dearly loved *(Colossians 3:12)*.

- I decree, and I declare I am God's Chosen, and I am blameless *(I Corinthians 1:8)*.

- I decree, and I declare I am set free as God's Chosen *(Romans 8:2; John 8:32)*.

- I decree, and I declare I am God's Chosen and

crucified with Christ *(Galatians 2:20)*.

- I decree and declare I am God's Chosen and a light in the world *(Matthew 5:14)*.

- I decree and declare I am God's Chosen and more than a conqueror *(Romans 8:37)*.

- I decree and declare I am God's Chosen and the righteousness of God *(2 Corinthians 5:21)*.

- I decree, and I declare I am God's Chosen, and I am safe *(I John 5:18)*.

- I decree, and I declare I am God's Chosen, and I am part of God's kingdom *(Revelation 1:6)*.

- I decree, and I declare I am God's Chosen, and I am healed from sin *(I Peter 2:24)*.

- I decree, and I declare I am God's Chosen, and I am no longer condemned *(Romans 8:1, 2)*.

- I decree, and I declare I am God's Chosen, and I am not helpless *(Philippians 4:13)*.

- I decree, and I declare I am an overcomer and God's Chosen *(I John 4:4).*

- I decree, and I declare I am persevering, and I am God's Chosen *(Philippians 3:14).*

- I decree, and I declare I am protected, and I am God's Chosen *(John 10:28).*

- I decree, and I declare I am born again, and I am God's Chosen *(I Peter 1:23).*

- I decree, and I declare I am God's Chosen and a new creation *(2 Corinthians 5:17).*

- I decree, and I declare I am God's Chosen, and I am delivered *(Colossians 1:13).*

- I decree, and I declare I am God's Chosen, and I am redeemed from the curse of the law *(Galatians 3:13).*

- I decree, and I declare I am God's Chosen and qualified to share in His inheritance *(Colossians*

1:12).

- I decree, and I declare I am God's Chosen and Victorious *(1 Corinthians 15:57)*

| CHAPTER 10 |

STAY CHOSEN

God has chosen you for a specific purpose. The calling He has for you can ONLY be fulfilled by you. Don't look at anyone and decide to do what they have been chosen to do. Ask God why He chose you and what His plans and purpose for your life are.

Before you were born, God chose you. He's already equipped you with everything you need to fulfill His calling on your life. He will use your unique abilities, divine talents, and sanctified personality for eternal purposes. He has chosen you to love difficult people, bring light to dark places, inject hope into hopeless situations, choose joy amid discouragement, live righteously amid compromise, pray for heaven to invade the earth, make hell smaller and heaven bigger, encourage the discouraged, pray for the sick and be a friend to the lonely.

Being reminded that God has chosen me in my

imperfections for His purposes and loves me even as I am is a great comfort to me. When I realized that the Creator of the Universe chose me, I began to understand there was no need for me to have a crisis of identity. I was designed in His image and created for His marvelous plans. In my confusion, chaos, failure, and blaming myself for making wrong choices, I realized that God doesn't choose perfect people. He just wants us to come as we are. The real challenge is to quiet the doubts in our minds long enough to hear and receive those three affirming words: "I CHOSE YOU" (John 15:16b). Jesus is calling you to be part of a greater team. You have not been overlooked, as you are fully seen by our All-Knowing God. Your brokenness, imperfections, and failures have not disqualified you from His purpose for you.

Disappointments and rejection will be a part of earthly life, but your unconditional worth in Jesus will never change. Even as you glance through the pages of this book, you may feel undeserving and inadequate. You may feel you're trying too hard or not trying hard enough. But this is a reminder that you are fully seen and known as our God, who is still in the business of using imperfect people for His perfect plan.

God's hand selects, in every generation, men and

women who are bold and audacious enough to serve Him wholeheartedly. God only requires your yes for service in His household. No matter how old we are, sometimes we're still that awkward child who needs to hear these words: "I chose you." We want to be the one selected, preferred, and hand-picked for a reason.

I wonder how Jesus' disciples felt when He said these powerful words to them in John 15:16a-b: *"You didn't choose me. I chose you."*

Our perfect Savior picked some of the most imperfect people to be a part of His team: a doubter (Thomas), a hothead (Peter), and a guy who had a full-time job profiting off his own people (Matthew). Most came from lowly, insignificant lives. They weren't the richest or most important. They were often overlooked. They were flawed, unrefined, and unqualified.

I'm sure they didn't feel like the best or most appropriate choice. Yet Jesus saw them fully and chose them anyway. And together, with Him, they changed the world. As a perfectionist, I feel like this seems too good to be true. But as a human being, I know it's a sigh of relief. "I chose you."

As I close the chapters of this book, I want to remind you that your gift is not just a talent but a divine blessing bestowed upon you by God. It's perfectly tailored and custom-made according to your personality and the way God crafted you. You can't work for your gift; you just discover it and receive it. You can use it to satisfy your flesh or use it to serve others. Embrace, nurture, and let it shine brightly in the world. Remember that every step you take, every challenge you face, is part of a greater purpose. Trust in the unique path laid out for you, and never underestimate the impact you can have. Your light is needed, and the world awaits your contribution.

The blessing of God is in His perfect will for your life. Provision is guaranteed, peace will flow like a river, and your energy will jump-start your day. The only thing that's perfect in your life is your assignment. God has a tailor-made suit for you. If you tried on someone else's, it would be too tight and vice versa. Many desire to do God's will but struggle because they're not sure what God's will is for them. Sometimes, we need to just stop and ask God to give us wisdom to discern His will.

There is something on the inside of you that God has placed there for you to be a world changer. The treasure that's in you is designed to bless the nations. After reading this book, I challenge you to be better so you can expect the greater. Jesus said we would do greater works than He did while He was here on earth. That means He has given you precisely what you need to release and manifest the potential that is within you.

You're not who everybody else says you are, you are becoming who you were meant to be. Get excited about your future! God wants you to walk in your greatness. Greatness arrives when you complete God's plan for your life and satisfy divine expectations. You will be unstoppable; you'll experience double grace, double favor, supernatural expansion, miracles, signs, and wonders as you walk into this new season of self-discovery. No good thing will God withhold from you as you walk uprightly with Him. You are CHOSEN and becoming the person you were meant to be. You will bear good fruit that shall remain.

Jesus, thank You for seeing us fully and loving us unconditionally. It's humbling to know You have chosen us to be in a relationship with You and to participate in Your Kingdom's work. Help us to silence any lies and listen only to Your calling in the Mighty Name of Jesus.

SALVATION PRAYER

Heavenly Father, I come to You admitting that I am a sinner *(Romans 3:23)*

Right now, I choose to turn away from my sins and ask You to cleanse me by Your blood of all unrighteousness. I believe Your Son, Jesus, died on the cross to take away my sins.

I also believe that He rose again from the dead so that I may be justified and made righteous through faith in Him *(Romans 6:23)*. I call upon the name of Jesus Christ to be the Savior and Lord of my life *(Acts 2:21)*.

I declare right now that I am a born-again child of God *(Romans 10:9-10)*. I am free from sin and full of the righteousness of God. I am saved in Jesus' Name. I choose to follow You and ask that You fill me with the Power of the Holy Spirit *(Luke 11:3)* in Jesus Mighty Name, Amen.

Pleasant Reading !!
God bless you immensely !!

www.ingramcontent.com/pod-product-compliance
Lightning Source LLC
Chambersburg PA
CBHW061759070526
44586CB00023B/2630